Morality and Conflict

Morality and Conflict

STUART HAMPSHIRE

Basil Blackwell

First published 1983
Basil Blackwell Publisher Limited
108 Cowley Road, Oxford OX4 1JF, England

British Library Cataloguing in Publication Data

Hampshire, Stuart
Morality and conflict.
1. Ethics
I. Title
170 BJ37

ISBN 0-631-13336-4

Typesetting by Oxford Verbatim Limited
Printed and bound in Great Britain
by Billings and Sons Ltd, Worcester.

Contents

Acknowledgements

I am grateful to the Committee of the Thank-Offering to Britain Fund and to the British Academy for the invitation to give the Thank-Offering to Britain Fund lectures for 1976, and to the Oxford University Press which originally published the lectures as *Two Theories of Morality* (1977) for the British Academy. Chapter 2 is an amended version of these lectures. Copies of the original lectures are available from the British Academy, 20–21 Cornwall Terrace, London NW1. I am grateful also to the electors at Cambridge who invited me to give the Leslie Stephen Lecture in 1972 and to the Cambridge University Press who published the lecture in *Public and Private Morality* (1978). Chapter 4 is a slightly shorter version of this lecture, and chapter 5 is based on an essay for this same book. 'Two Kinds of Explanation' was written for the volume of essays entitled *The Idea of Freedom* in honour of Sir Isaiah Berlin, published by Oxford University Press (1979) and edited by Alan Ryan. I am grateful to him, and to the Oxford University Press, for permission to republish this essay here. 'Morality and Convention' was written for *Utilitarianism and Beyond*, edited by Amartya Sen and Bernard Williams and published by Cambridge University Press in 1982. I thank them and the Cambridge University Press for permission to republish. I should mention also the very valuable support of the Guggenheim Foundation which gave me a Fellowship in 1968 when I was beginning to pursue these inquiries.

1

Introduction

This book reproduces a gradual movement of thought about the nature of morality. The long chapter 2 ('Two Theories of Morality') reviews the two classical accounts of morality which have always seemed to me the most plausible and the least shallow in the literature: Aristotle's and Spinoza's. In both theories the basis of morality is found principally in powers of mind that are common to all mankind. In both theories the improvement of human life is to come from improved reasoning; and in their different ways both theories stress a contrast between reason on one side and desire and passion on the other. Slowly, and by the stages here marked in the succeeding chapters, I have come to disbelieve that the claims of morality can be understood in these terms. I have found reasons to disbelieve that reason, in its recognized forms, can have, and should have, that overriding role in making improvements which these two philosophers allot to it. I argue in the later chapters that morality and conflict are inseparable: conflict between different admirable ways of life and between different defensible moral ideals, conflict of obligations, conflict between essential, but incompatible, interests. I believe now that the subject-matter of morality is misrepresented, and finally disappears from view, when a moralist concludes with a picture of the ideal human life and of a possible harmony of essential human interests, as Aristotle and Spinoza both did. I suggest reasons to disbelieve that there can be any such single ideal and any such ultimate harmony.

It will reasonably be objected that this path has been trodden many times and that it is late in history to make such discoveries. Nietzsche long ago denounced the classical tradition in ethics with its comfortable claims for reason and harmony. Not only that, but since Nietzsche much popular thinking has moved away decisively from claims for the possibility of rational theory in matters of moral concern; logical positivists and existentialists have had great and continuing influence outside academic circles, and their affirmations of the limits of reason in ethics are stale news. My answer is that in spite of Nietzsche the classical tradition of moral speculation is still of the greatest continuing value: the tradition, that is, of Plato, Aristotle, Spinoza, Hume, Kant, Mill, Sidgwick, Moore, Prichard, Ross, Rawls. It is easy to criticize the usual academic study of these authors, and of their theories, as being lifeless, pedantic, unreal, hopelessly abstract and naive, unimaginative, and depressingly tame. Undeniably there is a gap between the tone of discussions of moral philosophy in universities and the tone of discussions of particular moral problems as they are encountered in politics and in private life: a gap also between the imaginative presentation of moral realities in literature and their comparatively flat, abstract representation in academic philosophy. I believe that the comparatively flat and abstract arguments of moral philosophers are complementary to the more vivid presentation of particular cases in fiction and in history: both are needed in reflection on conduct and character. Reflection on the ends of action, and on the ultimate grounds of approval and remorse, must sometimes require generalization, a calm, clear tone, the marking of distinctions, objectivity, an academic style: even though the subject-matter cannot be exhausted by such inquiries, and even though it asks also for the vivid illustration by particular cases drawn from direct experience or from history. Nietzsche challenged the tradition of moral reasoning and of academic discussion of ethics, as Hegel had before him; but the tradition has survived the challenge, having absorbed much of the criticism and having probably benefited from it. As for logical positivism and existentialism, they were just incidents within the tradition, to be properly assessed by the tradition's internal standards of rationality.

The argument of this book, taken as a whole, is that there are two faces of morality: the rational and articulate side and the less than rational, the historically conditioned, fiercely individual, imaginative, parochial, the less than fully articulate, side. The chapters of this book try to show the two sides separately and detached from each other, which is obviously not as they are presented in our experience. In conduct, and in normal thinking about conduct from day to day, we naturally switch attention from one aspect of moral claims upon us to the other. The very general theories, applicable to all mankind, which make up the tradition of moral philosophy, certainly have flowed into, and formed, the habits of thought which in turn determine much of ordinary reasoning in politics, and ordinary reasoning about the issues of private life. Nietzsche's splendid rhetoric cannot undo these effects, nor can we reasonably unlearn and discard the abstract thought handed down to us. But the moral traditions of a particular, and historically conditioned, way of life are equally alive in our imagination and feelings.

Given the vast domain represented by the word 'morality', anything asserted about morality as a whole, if it is true at all, must be true only with many qualifications and exceptions. The whole conduct of life is at issue, as it has been viewed over the centuries and in many places. Therefore one can only reasonably hope to point to some connections in clear thinking about the conduct of life, connections that are essential and that seem to have been neglected in philosophy, or neglected recently; probably because a prevailing theory of knowledge, or a prevailing philosophy of mind, stands in the way. Chapter 3, 'Two Kinds of Explanation', is brought into the book because the distinction between the two aspects of morality cannot be made clear without a corresponding distinction between two kinds of answer which are available when an explanation of a human activity or practice is called for. The two aspects of morality, the universalizing and the particularizing, correspond to two modes of understanding and explaining, one that is characteristic of the natural sciences, and the other that is characteristic of historical and linguistic studies. An explanation of an activity or practice, and the justification of it in a context of moral inquiry, are certainly different things and must not be confused. But they are closely related when human activities are in question, in so far as the type of explanation that is available sets limits upon the type of justification that can reasonably be offered. For example, if a practice of mine can be adequately explained as the effect of my physical constitution, without any reference to my thoughts and feelings, the justification of the practice must assume a very different form than it would have had if the practice had been adequately explained as the outcome of my desires and calculations. This is only an extreme example of the relation between explanation and justification. A person engaging in an activity, and adopting a practice, often asks himself, and tries to explain, why he is doing it, as well as asking whether there are good reasons for his doing it, objectively considered. We often want to understand ourselves, and the considerations that are actuating us, before we decide what course to follow. The appropriate description of the activity or practice, appropriate in a moral context, often in part depends on the explanation of the agent's engagement in it; and the agent normally knows this. Not only this: the agent's belief about the explanation of his activity, even if the belief is not true, is sometimes relevant both to the description of the action and to the assessment of its moral quality. A person might believe that he is moved to action on a particular occasion by a strong, even overwhelming, impulse to correct his neighbour's misdeeds, while the better explanation of his action would mention his mood of irritable jealousy. The moral quality of his action, and even its proper description, is modified by the fact that he believes his action to be the outcome of a particular impulse and thought. The entanglement of justification with explanation arises from the agent's reflection on his own beliefs and desires, and on his own activities and practices; it arises from the reflexivity of the human mind, which is the topic of Chapter 3. The attribution of virtue or vice to a person because of a certain activity or practice involves some reference to the agent's state of mind; and his state of mind is in turn affected by his own view of the causes influencing and forming his state of mind.

A person asks himself, or is asked by another, a normative question about an activity in which he is engaged: 'Why do you think that you should do this?' This is a request for a justification of, or for a defence of, his activity or practice, and it is a question that any normally reflective person must put to himself very often in untrivial circumstances: is his conduct defensible in moral terms, decent, honourable, respect-worthy, useful all things considered, fair, or the reverse? Suppose that the agent says to himself, or to another: 'I engage in this activity because it has been the custom of my people, and I feel an intense loyalty to the customs of my family and country in this sphere.' Suppose the activity in question to be the disciplining and educating of children in a certain way. So far it seems that an explanation has been provided, but not a justification. Should a person allow his practice in this sphere to be determined by a sentiment of loyalty which he happens to feel? Why should he? Is a disposition of loyalty in this connection a virtue or a weakness? The implication of these last questions is that an argument is needed to establish what ought to be the practice, and to determine whether a person ought to be guided by a sentiment of loyalty; and this argument will be a justification, as contrasted with an explanation of fact.

The implication has not been misleading in the many cases where the agent on reflection sincerely replies with a utilitarian justification of preserving customs and carrying on traditions. It might be argued that it is useful, as making for general happiness and stability, that he acts upon this sentiment of loyalty to his people and their past. Alternatively, there might be some argument from unfairness: for example, that justice requires that a minority should be protected and supported through support of its inherited customs. This justification would be an appeal to some general principle of justice, corresponding to the general principle of utility. The thesis of the last two chapters of the book is that the presumed implication may sometimes be misleading, because there is no such move from explanation to justification by means of an argument that appeals to general moral principles; sometimes the justification is not to be found in this kind of rational structure, which has the twin principles of utility and of justice, however formulated, at its base. The justification is to be found, not in argument towards a general principle, but in the specification of a complex array of historical realities and causal relations of the kind which Kant called anthropological. The justification is not to be found in the utility of the particular conventions, customs and practices, or even in the utility, generally speaking, of having some such conventions, customs and practices. It is to be found in the fact that they have become an essential element in the subject's way of life.

At this point two oppositions, often accepted in contemporary philosophy as unquestionable, are being questioned: fact and value, and reason and sentiment. The argument in these last two chapters requires that sometimes, and with some moral concerns, the complex description of a whole way of life, and of its history, do fill the place occupied in other moral contexts by general principles of utility and justice: that is, the justification stops when the interconnections of practices and sentiments within a complete way of life are described. A way of life, adequately described and interpreted, is not exactly a fact, or an assembly of facts, if only because it can obviously be adequately described and interpreted in different ways from different perspectives; also because any description of it will contain theories used to interpret behaviour and social relations, and therefore the 'hardness' and definiteness suggested by the word 'fact' is lacking. Alongside repeated patterns of behaviour, a way of life includes admired ideal types of men and women, standards of taste, family relationships, styles of education and upbringing, religious practices and other dominant concerns.

I describe to myself, or to another, the way of life which is mine and I specify the contribution to it made by the practice or activity that is in question. If I did not follow this practice, such-and-such other practices, which are elements in my way of life, would be undermined and lose their hold upon me. The justification is in this sense holistic. I would need either to abandon the way of life to which I am now, whether by choice or circumstance, committed, or I would find that many of the other activities and practices, to which I am at present committed, have lost their significance, and my activities have come to seem incoherent and confused. I would find myself at odds with myself, because I would have removed a practice that is the presupposition of some of my other customs and habits. A person who justifies his practices in this historical style implicitly or explicitly presupposes, as a fact of his own experience, and also of history and anthropology, that every man and woman lives imbedded in some particular way of life, which is not the way of life of all persons: secondly, that ways of life are coherent totalities of customs, attitudes, beliefs, institutions, which are interconnected and mutually dependent in patterns that are sometimes evident and sometimes subtle and concealed. One cannot easily abstract the activity or practice from its setting in a complete way of life, and make one-to-one comparisons between activities and practices which are parts of different ways of life. The moral assessments that result from such comparisons will often be misleading. 'Are the modern, permissive sexual customs better or worse than the sexual customs of the typical Christian middle-class family in 1900?' is a question that obviously requires the background of normal, related activities and practices in the two societies to be filled in. In abstraction from their setting in a way of life such a set of customs and practices cannot be realistically assessed from a moral point of view, that is, with reference to the human virtues or defects which they engender and express.

Utilitarians will ask whether one or the other practice is likely to contribute more to general happiness and to the fulfilment of desires. To obtain a determinate answer they will have to presuppose some very general truths about human nature in the abstract or they will need to understand in detail the different ways of life; and the contribution of the customs to particular ways of life, and the rival merits of the ways of life as wholes, will need to be assessed. Certainly one can reasonably compare family customs, for example, or commercial and professional practices, from the standpoint of justice as fairness, and therefore from a moral standpoint. It might be concluded, for example, that a certain practice, with its injunctions and prohibitions, involved discrimination against women as such and was unfair and unjust, while a comparable practice in another society respected the rights of women, rights which in the name of fairness ought to be respected everywhere. This also is a legitimate appeal to general principle, and the same considerations apply as in the appeal to a general principle of utility. The evil of the unfairness must be balanced against a possible counterbalancing consideration: that the practice, taken as a whole, makes a contribution to the way of life, and is an essential element in it, and the comparative value of the way of life from a moral point of view must enter the balance.

There is a taint of naturalism in the derivation of values from facts that is suggested here and that many contemporary philosophers may find intellectually unacceptable and perhaps also morally repugnant. From the existence of an established way of life, and from the fact that a certain set of practices support that way of life and are indispensable within it, one certainly cannot derive an unconditional duty binding on anyone who enjoys that way of life to engage in those practices. One can derive only a qualified and conditional duty, a *prima facie* duty, to engage in those practices: conditional, first, upon possibly overriding considerations of justice or utility, conditional, secondly, upon an evaluation of the way of life in question, taken as a whole, as comparatively respect-worthy and as not morally repellent and destructive. The actual, well-established habits and institutions of normal men and women, revealed in their conduct and their language, are good evidence about human nature, that is, of common human aspirations, needs and dispositions. The justification, therefore, is by an appeal to human nature, as revealed in history, not to a human nature as studied by biologists and psychologists. We can and do apply to these evidences criticism derived from general principles of fairness and utility, having in mind an attainable improvement of habits and institutions. But we know well that habits and institutions which are now reasonably criticized as grossly unfair and unjust – for example, in the relations between rich and poor – were not criticized by our ancestors in this way, partly because, imbedded in a different way of life, our ancestors had different targets for criticism from the standpoint of justice, and needed to imagine, or to anticipate, a different way of life, if they were to see the then prevailing relations between rich and poor as grossly unjust. Our descendants will criticize, from the standpoint of justice and utility, habits and institutions which to us seem scarcely alterable features of human nature as we know it. In reality many of them are just essential features of particular ways of life. In 'The Idea of a Perfect Commonwealth' and elsewhere Hume alludes to this alternation between the universalizing and principled aspect of our moralities, which engender a picture of the perfectly just and beneficent person and the perfectly just and beneficent society, and, on the other hand, 'the second nature' of a person living in a customary society, attached to the moral concerns that arise from comparatively local and temporary conditions. Characteristically, Hume keeps a balance between both aspects of human intelligence, the abstract or (in his terms) 'philosophical', and the historical.

If it is admitted that there are two significantly distinct kinds of explanation in the human sciences, as chapter 3 argues, are there correspondingly two significantly distinct kinds of justification in moral contexts? Chapters 6 and 7 argue that there are. It is the historical justification that incurs the reproach of being naturalistic, in the special sense that it derives an 'ought' from an 'is', a value from a complex set of facts. 'This is the approved practice of the people to whom I belong, and to whom I am committed, and I find nothing harmful in it': 'This is an essential part of the way of life to which I am committed and it is not an evil way of life': 'This has always been our practice, and, properly understood, it is not unfair, and it is important in our way of life': This is how I feel, and how I have always felt: to change now would be to repudiate my past, and I find nothing unjust or harmful in the practice.' These are justifications in a moral context, all of which appeal to the agent's sense of his own identity and character as a person and of his history, which partially determines his sense of identity. It is to be noted that the appeal is not to the necessity of having some established convention or rule, no matter what, as with traffic rules; the moral claim rests on attachment to these particular rules with their particular history and associations. This is Hume's 'second nature', within which men are naturally bound by their moral sentiments, while they are also attached by their moral sentiments to general principles of justice and benevolence: 'This is my ground and I must stand on it: I do not claim that everyone everywhere must do what I must do: but this is my character, and, because it is, I must act in this way.' Such justifications are sometimes spoken of as appeals to integrity, a distinct virtue to be ranked with justice and benevolence. In my essay 'Sincerity and Single-Mindedness' (*Freedom of Mind and Other Essays*, Oxford University Press 1972), I considered the wholeness of mind and purpose which is called integrity. But I believe that the justifications just cited can be as well understood within Hume's framework. The point of such historical replies to the call for justification – 'Why should I?' – lies in the refusal to rationalize the activity or practice beyond a certain point, and an acknowledgment of the particularity of the particular case. To represent integrity as a general human virtue, alongside justice and benevolence, might perhaps obscure this insistence on the particular and on the limits of rational argument. The justification rests on a feature of human nature that we know *a posteriori* to be no less general than a concern with happiness and with fairness: the multiplicity and diversity of the local and historical attachments that give sense to a normal person's life, alongside the common concerns of all men and women.

These issues have been muddled by the old faculty psychology, still retained by Hume, which distinguishes at this point between the part played by reason and the part played by the passions in ethics. Admittedly justifications that appeal to principles of justice and to utility permit more explicit and more prolonged argument than most justifications that appeal to convention and to history and to a story of personal commitment; it is often difficult, and sometimes perhaps impossible even, to spell out very explicitly the grounds for a sentiment of loyalty, for example, which constrains one to acknowledge duties and obligations that cannot be justified by general principles. Conduct that is neither unjust nor harmful may be dishonourable and disloyal, in view of the history of those involved, and it may be difficult to explain exactly what makes the act impossible with the precision that one might bring to arguments about injustice or harmfulness. But the sentiments and attitudes that are involved in such moral concerns are not blind excitements that just happen to occur; their reasonableness or unreasonableness is discussed and argumentatively examined, parallel cases compared, and the coherence of one sentiment with another tested. The arguments that come up when a person reflects on his ungeneralized moral sentiments are usually not as structured as utilitarian calculations of benefit and harm; but they are susceptible of being evaluated as reasonable or unreasonable, clear or confused. Moral sentiments can be adopted, endorsed and repudiated as a consequence of reflection.

In chapters 6 and 7 I am arguing for the equivalent in ethics of the principle that has to be recognized in the theory of knowledge: that all perception of the external world is from a particular point of view, and the observer must take account of his particular standpoint; he must not think of himself as standing beyond the rim of the world, observing it from the outside, as though he were a transcendent being; this is part of the argument in chapter 3. Similarly one ought not to think of oneself as adhering only to claims that are binding on all persons everywhere, and one ought not to leave out of account the particular standpoint, the local attachments, the peculiar history which are one's own. If one does think of duties and obligations wholly in terms of universal principles, one will either be deceiving oneself and failing to notice that one also acts upon other kinds of moral claim: alternatively, and much less probably, one will have harshly simplified one's conduct, as utilitarians propose, allowing only the virtue of benevolence which, isolated and alone, would be a rather bleak and inhuman virtue. Parts of Kant's *Critique of Judgement* are expounded in chapter 7 because Kant there argues that there is a middle domain between the laws of physics and universally binding moral law; though he confines this middle domain to aesthetics. I argue that the whole of what we call culture, including many of our moral beliefs and attitudes, falls within this middle realm.

2

Two Theories of Morality

1

Aristotle and Spinoza's moral philosophies, which are theories of practical reasoning and of human improvement, have seemed to me the most credible and the most worth developing of all moral theories in the light of modern knowledge and of contemporary philosophy. But they give very different accounts both of practical reason and of the improvement of human life at which practical reason should aim. They are competitors, and one cannot easily think of one theory as complementary to the other; rather one has finally to choose between them. The principal point of divergence between them is their opposing view of the relation between moral theory and ordinary, established moral opinions. Aristotle states clearly that moral theory must be in accord with established opinions and must explain these opinions as specifications of more general principles. An unphilosophical man of experience, who is of good character, usually reasons correctly on practical matters. Therefore Aristotle argues that acceptable moral theory will give a firm foundation to the principles that normally guide the decisions of the men whom we normally admire. Acceptable theory will not undermine established moral opinions nor bring about a systematic moral conversion.

By contrast, Spinoza in the *Ethics* claims to be showing the path to a necessary moral conversion which philosophical and moral theory introduce. As physical theory reveals a new world of particles in motion behind the ordinarily perceived world of medium-sized objects, so psychology and the philosophy of mind reveal a new psychic reality behind the ordinarily perceived passions and behind our ordinary purposes. Admittedly, most of our ordinary moral opinions are reaffirmed after the conversion; but a few of them are wholly repudiated, as depending on a false theory of the mind and on a false metaphysics. Those that are reaffirmed are supported by entirely different reasons; and practical reasoning is entirely reformed after the philosophical enlightenment. Therefore one can speak of two models of morality, which are opposed in their views both of the methods of ethics and of the prospects of human improvement.

2

It is now possible both to think and to write about morality without epistemological and logical barriers being placed between the original subject-matter of ethics – 'How ought we to live?' – and the reader who wants some direct or indirect answer to this question. The barriers have now been taken away, or have just gradually melted away; the barriers from epistemology and from the philosophy of logic and from the philosophy of language; the shibboleths of empiricist philosophy which represented the 'language' of ethics as a special subject of study. In 1949 I argued against that Humean theory of knowledge which obstructed discussion of morality in an article, 'Fallacies in Moral Philosophy', which was essentially a defence of Aristotle's methods in ethics (see my *Freedom of Mind and Other Essays*, Oxford University Press 1972). The barriers in the theory of knowledge, which came from Hume and Russell, were at that time complicated, at least in Britain, by a fascination, first, with the single modal word 'ought', and, secondly, with G. E. Moore's famous argument about the word 'good' in *Principia Ethica*.

Few philosophers now subscribe to a theory of belief that excludes the possibility of there being beliefs about good and bad, right and wrong, which have respectable and intelligible grounds no less than beliefs of other familiar kinds. As for the word 'ought', the study of modal words shows that the word 'ought' has no particular connection with morality, but rather that practical reason of any kind involves the use of a whole panoply of modal words, of which 'must' and 'ought' are probably the most interesting. As for the word 'good', exhaustive inquiries into semantics and into practical reasoning have ensured that the word 'good' will no longer be segregated as belonging to some peculiar kind of discourse, or as indicating some peculiar speech-act. The thought that something is good, or the belief that it is, or the doubt whether it is, will be accepted as being normal thoughts, normal beliefs and normal doubts, whether in moral contexts or elsewhere.

The way is therefore open to looking for the underlying structure of one's own beliefs in the area marked by the word 'moral', without embarrassment about the logical form of the sentences in which such beliefs are typically expressed.

3

Two points arise about the phrase 'the underlying structure of one's moral beliefs'; this structure is something that one may look for and yet may fail to find, not only because one is not ingenious enough to find it, but perhaps also because it may not be there to be found. It is always logically possible that one's beliefs, in this area as in others, are too unrelated to each other, and that they exhibit too little coherence, to be subsumed under any sufficiently small, even if complex, set of more general propositions. In this case there would be nothing that could properly be called an underlying structure of belief. Then one's moral beliefs would, at the least, be ill thought out, and at the worst would be incoherent, and in need of revision. Secondly, a person's moral beliefs could turn out to be highly complex, and not susceptible of being subsumed under any relatively short list of general principles of which they are instances; and yet they could still be said to have a structure, if some clear account could be given of why they are complex in one particular way, and if some pattern can be discerned in the relations between the elements. Reflection on moral intuitions may not result in a relatively simple theory which satisfactorily, if roughly, explains the intuitions as derivable from more general principles. Rather it may result in a theory which explains why no such simple theory is to be found, and why no such simple derivations are to be expected.

The second point touches the phrase 'one's moral beliefs' and its interpretation. I interpret this to mean my own intuitions and beliefs, after they have been corrected by reflection and in so far as I consider them not to be merely thoughtless reactions, and in so far as they have that degree of explicitness that justifies the use of the word 'belief'. It is not reasonable to assume a very great coincidence of moral belief between contemporaries who have different metaphysical and religious beliefs. There must be a divergence in some moral beliefs between contemporary and similarly educated Christians, Catholic or Evangelical, and on the other side Marxists and atheists. Even if there is a large area of agreement in the reasoned moral opinions of such persons, there must be crucial, sharp disagreements of a very untrivial kind. Not only this: but within a single lifetime a person may pass through more than one large reversal of moral opinion, and be converted from one set of moral beliefs to another. It is usual for people's moral beliefs to change, and even to change fundamentally, between adolescence and old age. A change in philosophical beliefs, either in the philosophy of mind or in the theory of knowledge, may well be a reason, or even the reason, for a moral conversion, and for a radical overhauling of his moral outlook. The normal situation is that a rational person hopes through reflection to clarify his own beliefs by finding in them a degree of coherence which had not been evident to him before he clarified them.

Perhaps the hidden coherence takes the form of a belief that his actions should have a constant tendency towards producing some identifiable consequence, not previously isolated in the subject's mind; or perhaps it takes the form of a very general principle of justice that makes an otherwise miscellaneous set of moral prohibitions into an intelligible set of instances. The subject then may understand for the first time why he thinks as he does on a variety of moral questions which had not been brought together in his mind before. The clarification of intuitions, and the discovery of connections between them, are likely to lead one to revise some moral opinions which have previously been uncriticized. As Aristotle argued, there is a two-way traffic by which intuitions are modified by reflection on the general principles that explain them, and the general principles are qualified by particular cases that do not fit and fall under them. Aristotle therefore claimed that there is a strong practical interest, a guide to action, in moral theory. For example, he who convinces himself that some form of utilitarianism is the theory that comes closest to his moral intuitions has, from then onwards, a more definite and well-demarcated target to aim at. If I have gradually convinced myself, as in fact I have, that there is an irreducible plurality of moral necessities constituting, first, an order of priority among necessary dispositions, and, secondly, a way of life that is to be aimed at, I again have a more definite vision of what my intuitions have been pointing to. This has practical effects in my thought about political and personal problems. One has only fifty or so years to think, and to act on one's conclusions, if like Aristotle one excludes the possibility of moral coherence in childhood.

4

Specific moral opinions – for example, that torture ought not to be used, or must never be used, in the interrogation of terrorists, even if it saves lives and prevents more suffering – are often called moral intuitions, when stress is being laid on the unreflective, unphilosophical character of the opinions; and this is a standard and correct use of the word 'intuitions'. Beliefs that can be called intuitions are far from being peculiar to morality, and there is nothing questionable or irrational in having beliefs which are intuitions and which one then seeks to clarify and explain, in the sense of 'explain' already indicated. Beliefs that are intuitions are the natural product of unanalysed experience working on a mind that is adapted to making discriminations of a kind which the organism regularly needs to make. Recognition of perceived objects as being of a certain size is an obvious case of belief or knowledge which is usually intuition, as is also recognition of persons and re-identification of many other types of individuals. When you ask a person why he believes that it was so-and-so's voice that he heard, and what makes him think that it was, the belief is not normally discredited, nor made to appear irrational, if it turns out that he has no clear idea of why he thought so, or why he now thinks so, or of how he discriminated: that is, if he has no clear idea of the mechanism of discrimination and identification, and of those perceptual clues which would be studied in the psychology of perception, and which have in fact been used by him. The belief is not discredited unless people in general are unsuccessful, except when they can adequately explain their beliefs in this sphere by reference to their explicitly formulated grounds.

There are vast areas of belief necessary to survival within which intuition is not discreditable, and in which the mind operates by a mechanism of causes and effects normally unknown to the thinking subject and not easily open to his inspection. If it were possible to count beliefs, one could say that most of one's beliefs about the environment are of this character, being unsupported by conscious reasoning and even unsupported by reasoning which, though not conscious, is later traceable by reflection. My mind has been set to respond to certain clues with appropriate expectations and with beliefs, usually true beliefs, about the nature of the objects before me. It is admittedly always an advantage for me to know how my beliefs are caused, because I thereby acquire the means of methodically making corrections on occasions when the available clues are liable to mislead me. If a person understands the mechanism, he knows how it might go wrong, and he can take precautions not to assent to the beliefs that he would naturally form in deceiving circumstances. But Nature has not left it entirely to us to form beliefs by the conscious exercise of powers of inference in the sphere of recognition of objects and of persons, at least in the normal cases. The abbreviated inferences, which we may call intuitions, happen without the subject's being aware of the successive steps in the pre-conscious inference. Such pre-conscious inferences guide not only recognitions and discriminations but also actions and manipulations. The compressed reasoning, which is the core of every practical skill exercised regularly and rapidly, can occasionally be brought to the surface and spelt out, when we are asked why we made on the instant the choice that we did – the immediate choice: 'Because I thought that the ball would bounce the other way.'

Aristotle explicitly makes the comparison between perceptual judgements, of the kind that constitute recognitions, and moral intuitions, that is, immediate, unreflective moral judgements of the form – 'this ought not to be done' or 'this kind of thing cannot be done; it is impossible.' I am arguing that it is a valid comparison in at least one important respect: in the relation between the belief that *p* and knowing why one believes that *p*. An experienced and consistently reliable observer is often not skilful in making explicit, either for the benefit of himself or for the benefit of others, why he believes that *p*, or skilful in isolating the more general principle that explains his beliefs. It is an advantage, even from a practical standpoint, for the subject to know the answer to the question 'why?' when his intuitions are questioned; and it is an advantage, even from a practical standpoint, for a person to have the ability to state the more general principle, or principles, which explain why he comes to the conclusions that he does in fact reach intuitively, and by compressed and pre-conscious inference.

The ability to say why, and to explain his conclusion, is a distinct intellectual talent, which has the great advantage of making occasional sources of error and of confusion evident, or at least traceable. An explicit criterion is available which was not available before; this makes deliberate planning possible, and, as Aristotle puts it, gives one a target at which to aim. Without a formulation of explicit principles, which gives one something definite to aim at, one is groping towards the target in the dark and one can be more easily misled by muddled conceptions of the end in view. The intuition turns out to be mere prejudice, and the explanation of my belief may turn out to be no kind of justification of it. Similarly, the games-player's reason for playing the stroke that he did may on reflection be exposed as a bad reason, and, independently, the stroke may be shown to be a mistake, the product of a bad habit. But in neither case does this count as a reason for distrusting intuitions as a general policy; there is reason to check habits of thought by reflection.

It may be objected that the Aristotelian analogy between perceptual intuitions and moral intuitions is imperfect and that it conceals important differences. It does. One expects a man's moral intuitions to be explained by comparatively few general principles which constantly enter into the abbreviated inferences. One even expects the explanatory general principles to cohere in some kind of order or grouping so that, taken together, they constitute a morality which is intelligible as a whole: intelligible as constituting a consistent plan of life, or as presenting a realizable ideal of conduct, in a normal span of life and in a normal setting, or as singling out a few achievements as supremely desirable before all others. But the principles that explain the formation of this or that perceptual belief are vastly diverse, and there is no requirement that they should form an intelligible whole. The analogy is helpful only in so far as it draws attention to one complex common feature of the two kinds of judgement and belief: that the judgements are often immediately made, normally without a conscious process of inference, and the complicated steps towards the conclusion may be reconstructed, either through the subject's reflection or by experiment or by some combination of the two. Therefore one can say about moral intuitions that theory may lie behind them, and yet they may be made without conscious thought or argument, as if they were immediate identifications of persons or things. The theory may be contained in the habit of reasoning from certain grounds to certain conclusions and not in explicit assertions rehearsed and present to the mind.

The thought that enters into one's moral judgements may be elaborate thought, and yet be inaccessible to the subject. Consider a case: suppose that one is sure that one must make a rule against the use by the army and police of techniques of interrogation of terrorists that amount to mental torture, and *a fortiori* against physical torture, and that this rule must be enforced, whatever the costs. Sensory deprivation is one form of mental torture, or near torture. Suppose that one might save many lives by finding a bomb in a public place and that this method of interrogation by sensory deprivation would be effective. Why do I think that the utilitarian judgement would be wrong in this case? It is not an emotional reaction, I think, but a reasonable judgement. Can I have a reason without knowing what it is? I might say 'Yes, that is my reason', when it is suggested to me. If Aristotle was right about the analogy with perception, I can have a reason without immediately knowing what it is.

Certainly it is more than useful, it is even necessary, that I should discover what the reason is that makes me think that it would be wrong to employ near torture, sensory deprivation, in interrogation of terrorists, wrong when even this is virtually certain to avert more suffering than is involved in the near torture. Perhaps there is a reason which, when exposed, will no longer appear to me a sufficient reason, or even a good reason. To repeat: the advantage is with conscious thought and argument, which allows for reflection and for evaluation and for checking of the unseen mechanisms of thought and for open discussion of these mechanisms. I may recognize, as a matter of fact causal judgement, that so-and-so is the reason which has been influencing me; but at the same time I may recognize that it is a bad reason, and therefore my opinion changes on reflection.

5

The word 'theory' has different connotations in the phrase 'moral theory' and in 'scientific theory'. In both cases 'theory' stands for a set of propositions, comparatively general ones, which explain a much larger, sometimes heterogeneous range of accepted propositions that seem to be more unrelated to each other than they really are. I use the word 'propositions' widely here to include instructions and prohibitions and rules. But moral theory, like any practical theory and theory of action, does not purport to be accurate in the sense in which a scientific theory must be accurate if it is to be acceptable at all. A moral theory is not necessarily, or even usually, falsified by a clear and indisputable negative instance. It is sufficient, as Aristotle remarked, that the moral theory, and the set of more or less general propositions that compose it, should turn out to be acceptable for the most part and on the whole, in actual experience, political and private. Suppose that one takes a conventional grammar of the Latin (or French or English) language as being a theory of the speech habits of the speakers of the language: one will expect there to be exceptions, some listed and some not, to the general rules of grammar and of word order formulated in the theory. Some of the exceptions will be not only listed, but explained, and some will be left as mere anomalies. Knowing the grammar will help a native speaker of the language, who has learnt to speak the language without the grammar; the grammar will help him to decide what is correct in doubtful cases, and it will be a guide to correct speech. Concurrently, actual speech and writing, in which he follows his intuitions of correctness, will occasionally lead him to revise the grammar that he had accepted hitherto as correct. Some exceptions will lead him to reject a rule that he had previously considered correct as a rule of grammar. Other exceptions will simply stand as odd exceptions, which are compatible with the rule holding for the most part and on the whole; there is a circle of mutual correction between practice and normative theory.

This type of theory – or, if you prefer, theory in this sense of the word – obviously contains propositions which are different in their logical relations to each other from the propositions that constitute a scientific theory. But it is very far from being a deviant and exceptional type of theory, or from involving a deviant sense of the word 'theory'. The distinction between theory and practice is as pervasive and important an opposition as that between theory and observation, or between theory and fact. Every worthwhile game, craft or art has its theory, which stands in opposition to its practice; and in most games, crafts and arts the relation between theory and practice, and the relation between knowledge of theory and excellence in practice, are controversial matters, as they have been in moral philosophy from its known beginnings in Plato and Aristotle. Is the man of experience and knowledge of the world who also has good dispositions by nature, generally to be preferred, as a regular source of sound judgement, to the man who has reflected on moral theory and who has arrived at sound conclusions at an abstract and theoretical level? Analogous questions are asked about other practical theories, for example, in games and crafts. The closest analogy for ethics has often seemed to be the relation between theory and practice in the fine and applied arts, though this analogy is far from being perfect; and the relation itself obviously differs significantly in the various different arts. There is a requirement that moral theory should exhibit a degree of coherence and comparative clarity, while this kind of constraint is not generally imposed on the very various theories that are put into practice in the imaginative and free or liberal arts – in the arts of music, painting and poetry, for instance. Secondly, a moral theory makes claims to be exclusively valid and not to be considered as just one of a number of equally valid or possible theories. Aesthetic theories concerned with works of the imagination are not generally taken to be to the same extent exclusive and competitive with each other.

6

The elements of moral theory that I have distinguished in chapter 4 and in 'Ethics: a Defence of Aristotle' (*Freedom of Mind and Other Essays*, Oxford University Press 1972), and that need to be more fully analysed are: the conception of an imagined best way of life, together with a conception of the specific virtues that are essential in it, and of some order of priority among these virtues: priority, that is, in the desirability of these virtues, and in the weight that is given to them in the overall assessment of a line of conduct or of a policy, and also in comment on the character of a person and on his actions. That is the first element, still Aristotelian. All moral theories, which we would consider seriously, imply, when they do not explicitly state, a more or less precise conception of what virtues a man must have if he is to be praised in an unqualified way as a human being, and imply also an order of priority among these virtues; and they either imply or state a rather definite conception of the best way of life, and of the several distinct dispositions and interests which this admired and sought after way of life will satisfy. The conception of a way of life has to include some social ideal, more or less detailed, depending on the priority that is given to political activities and to social usefulness. It includes also habits of behaviour and manners, observances, rituals of behaviour, which are not so much direct expressions of explicit moral beliefs as expressions of unstated moral attitudes and which can often only be identified with difficulty. The term 'way of life' has to be vague if only because it represents not only explicit ideals of conduct, deliberately chosen, but also ideals which have not been made explicit, or formulated, and which may be expressions of not fully conscious preferences, feelings, and ambitions.

This three-tiered theoretical framework – injunctions, order of virtues, way of life – is to be defended and justified in the same way that all theories have to be defended and justified: that it systematizes, and thereby explains, the moral intuitions which I share with many other men less incompletely than any other theory does. Secondly, the theory can find a place within the framework, and it can therefore explain, other and conflicting theoretical frameworks which cannot in their turn find a place for it. Other theories of morality – Hume's theory, Kant's theory, utilitarian theory, for instance – can be expressed within this framework, as precribing ways of life which give differing priorities to essential virtues and to differing powers of mind and habits of action. These rival and non-Aristotelian theories are naturally not best expressed in Aristotelian terms, because these terms will not exhibit the grounds, external to ethics and drawn from epistemology and logic, on which the rival theories rest. But their substantial moral content can be expressed in Aristotelian terms.

Proceeding from the most vague general elements of the moral framework theory to the more particular, one comes to the first element, to moral prohibitions, the injunctions and judgements that exclude types of action, or forms of conduct, which must not be performed or into which a man must not enter; and these judgements and injunctions may apply also to attitudes and purposes which a man must not, or more weakly, ought not, to have. The notion of moral prohibition, of what must not be done, of barriers and of restraint of vice or defect, may be more weakly expressed, in accordance with the general use of these modal words, as that which ought not to be. But it is a mistake, introduced by some post-Kantian moralists, to think of 'ought' as the primary, or even as a primary, constituent of moral injunctions and prohibitions. The strong moral prohibition is most naturally expressed as 'I must not' and the injunction as 'You must'. This is not only a feature of speech and of the public expression of the thought. It is also true that the thought which is naturally expressed as 'I must do this' is a different thought from that which is expressed as 'I ought to do this.' Some actions, and some omissions of action, are impossible, out of the question, and not to be further considered, and they are impossible from a moral point of view, as contrasted, for example, with a legal impossibility.

Our moral intuitions, however acquired, present us with a large number of prohibitions of types of conduct, types of action that must not be performed, because they are wrong, morally repugnant, shocking, indefensible, inhuman, vicious, disgraceful. Reflecting on these intuitions in a critical spirit, and constantly looking for some simple connection between them, I ultimately find that they are not instances of one, or instances of a very few, much more general prohibitions or injunctions. They are irreducibly plural, and they single out various types of serious wrong-doing and despised conduct which are to be avoided. They are various, irreducibly plural, for the same reasons that the virtues and vices are plural; namely, that the ways of life which men aspire to and admire and wish to enjoy are normally a balance between, and combination of, disparate elements; and this is so, partly because human beings are not so constructed that they have just one overriding concern or end, one overriding interest, or even a few overriding desires and interests. They find themselves trying to reconcile, and to assign priorities to, widely different and diverging and changing concerns and interests, both within the single life of an individual, and within a single society. They find themselves divided in their admirations and in their goals and they attach value to activities and dispositions which they know are normally incompatible, or which cannot easily be combined, or which cannot, under presently existing circumstances, be combined at all; even if it may sometimes be true that under better circumstances, and perhaps theoretically attainable ones, the activities could be combined. They also admire, and pursue, virtues which could not be combined without abridgement in any imaginable world: for instance, spontaneity and scrupulous care, integrity and political skill in manœuvre. Serious moral problems typically take the form of balancing strict but conflicting requirements, which Plato dramatized in the *Republic* by representing the man educated to be just as educated to combine and balance gentleness and firmness. As there must be conflicts in society, so there must be conflicts in the soul, and it is the same virtue that strikes the right balance in situations of conflict.

The conflicts between different virtues – justice and kindness, loyalty and fairness, honesty and the will to please – are paralleled, inevitably, by conflicts between prohibitions. I find myself in a situation in which I cannot both obey the injunction 'You must always support your friend when he needs your support' and 'One cannot be biased where justice is in question.' I have to weigh the relative weight which ought to be given to these now conflicting moral claims in the particular circumstances in which they have presented themselves. But this weighing is not a process of which no account can be given. On the contrary the reasons for thinking that, in the particular circumstances of the case, one claim overrides the other can be spelt out; and these reasons follow a certain general pattern, a pattern that invokes a way of life, and, subordinate to this, invokes an order of priority among the virtues and interests recognized as constitutive of this way of life. He who is able to tell you why he subordinates one of these claims to the other will not avoid disclosing his ranking of different types of human performance as more or less to be sought after and admired, and therefore as better or worse. He has in mind an ordering of dispositions and interests, which is an ordering of virtues.

Moral ideas are naturally first introduced and learnt by a child as a set of imperatives, seeming to be irreducibly plural and with reasons that are more obscure and less evident than the simple imperatives themselves. Becoming adult certainly entails looking for the reasons that lie behind the accepted imperatives and it entails questioning their apparent disconnection. The search for connections may end in several different ways: among others in the recognition of an order of priority among competing virtues, and in the recognition of complexity in ideals; and therefore in a recognized need, often recurring, to strike a balance at all three levels; first between conflicting moral claims, which may be rights, duties or obligations, and secondly, between conflicting virtues, and, thirdly, between conflicting elements in a complex way of life which is sought after.

A defence of irreducible plurality is needed of a more systematic and philosophical kind, if hedonists, utilitarians of all kinds, and ideal contract theorists are to be rationally challenged. The defence must not try to show that utilitarianism and hedonism are untenable first-order moral opinions because they are logically incoherent; this would be to try to prove too much. He who believes that the discriminating, and reasonably altruistic, pursuit of pleasure and prevention of suffering is the only way of life worth pursuing is not so far involved in a logical confusion. If he is confused at all, he is confused about his reasons for believing that certain specific practices are wrong: perhaps about why he hates injustice, or about why he would not commit the crime of murder in almost any circumstances, or about why he admires honesty and loyalty as much as he probably does. If he has been thoroughly tested by actual and imaginary examples, and he has successfully shown that the balance of pleasure over pain, or the prevention of suffering, or the maximum satisfaction of preferences, are in all cases the only relevant considerations for him, one would have to admit that his moral beliefs were so far coherent and not confused. The criticism of them would have to move to a different level. One line of reflection, which might be persuasive, would stress the actual variety of conflicting ends which we know that intelligent men have had in view at different times and in different places, and which he has left out of account: an appeal to his imagination of possibilities which he may have overlooked or failed to understand.

Perhaps the case for recognizing an irreducible plurality of occasionally conflicting moral claims can be made stronger by an *a priori* argument. The proposal of a single criterion of moral judgement, as by utilitarians, is also a simplification of the virtues; all the virtues must be directly or indirectly derived from the two central virtues of active benevolence and active beneficence. The disposition to be fair and just is to be shown to be praiseworthy, in so far as those who have this disposition are likely, because of the disposition, to be more than usually beneficent; and similarly for all the other virtues. Those who find themselves compelled, in a particular case, to choose between justice and kindness, or between respect for the freedom for the individual and concern for the safety of the individual, have a computational problem; will a preferable outcome, on the whole, flow from preserving the freedom of the individual in these circumstances rather than from protecting the individuals against death and misfortune? A murderous disposition is dreaded, not because of the act of murder which is threatened, but because of the unhappiness and suffering that are the threatened consequences of the murder.

Adopting the contrary and Aristotelian theory, one may stress the conflict between duties and between prohibitions of other kinds, when one is thinking of conduct as expressing the character and dispositions of a man; also when one is thinking of a set of actions as expressions of a man's purposes, interests, and sentiments, and when one is describing and evaluating them from this internal point of view. In the common vocabulary actions are sometimes classified and discriminated by their outcomes and effects, and sometimes by the desires and purposes which they manifest, and sometimes from both points of view. A moralist who singles out 'the nature and quality of the act', as opposed to its likely or actual consequences, is probably thinking of the difference between killing a man and murdering him, between murdering and assassinating, between killing and letting die, between theft and fraud, between terrorizing and torturing, between lying and misleading, and so on; and he is probably thinking of the conventional and institutional classification of actions, which may be distinguished as a third type of classification, alongside classification by consequences and classification by disposition manifested, even though these types are not always distinct and are often combined in a single action description. There is, for example, the human institution, historically recognized, of the assassination of tyrants; and therefore the killing of Hitler by the July Conspirators, had it occurred, would have been described as assassination rather than as murder, in a context in which the rightness or wrongness of the act was in question. The question 'Is assassination ever justified?' is a different question from 'Is murder ever justified?'.

Turning back to the previous example of sensory deprivation as a means of interrogating prisoners who are terrorists, one may raise the same moral question in three distinguishable ways. First, are the effects of this treatment of prisoners, both immediate and remote effects, so bad as to outweigh the probable good effects, and therefore ought the practice to be prevented? Secondly, is this treatment of prisoners so cruel and callous as to be morally repugnant and therefore to be prevented? Thirdly, does sensory deprivation amount to a form of torture of prisoners and ought it therefore to be prevented because all torture ought to be prevented, in virtue of the nature and quality of the act, an act intrinsically repugnant and an outrage? Most actions are at once the bringing about of an effect, also the manifestation of the desires and purposes of the particular agent, and also must be labelled as being of a certain recognized and institutionalized kind. A single criterion morality, such as classical utilitarianism, deliberately makes an abstraction from standard action descriptions as morally irrelevant except as indicating consequences, and utilitarianism particularly disregards institutional descriptions, and also descriptions of actions in terms of the motives and of the feelings expressed.

The single criterion, proposed by utilitarians, for deciding between conflicting moral claims finally makes all choices into a choice between various ways of ensuring a single result. These different paths to a single destination are to be understood, and their differences justified, as suiting the needs and interests of persons and communities with different histories and therefore in different situations. The apparent diversity of goals and of moral concerns is to be explained either by superstition or, in rational, free-thinking people, by the different utilities to be attached to the same virtues in different circumstances. The choice that one may seem to have to make at a moment of crisis and conflict is not, on reflection, to be counted as a choice between two irreducibly different ways of life so much as a calculation of the efficacy of the superficially different ways of life in producing the unavoidably preferred result; not a choice between ultimately diverging paths, but between routes that converge finally.

These implications of the no conflict, single criterion moral theory may be accepted by the theory's reflective supporters without qualms. Perhaps the argument against the single criterion should then be pressed further and made more general. That there should be conflicting moral claims, which are not to be settled by appeal to a criterion that is always overriding and final, may be represented as a consequence of the nature of practical choice for a language-using, and vocabulary-choosing and vocabulary-creating, creature. Such a creature has the means to present to himself alternative futures, either in specific or in vague terms, extending over long or short periods of time. He has the means to hope for, or to dread, tomorrow, next month, next year, middle age, old age, his own weakness or his recovery from weakness. He unavoidably thinks about his immediate and middle-distance future and he has intentions in respect of them. He knows many things that he will be doing soon, and at some time, and he knows when he will be doing some of them very exactly. The terms in which he thinks of his future vary with his social position, his temperament and interests, and his moral beliefs. He can choose for himself the terms in which he will both present to himself, and plan, his own probable future, and possible futures: within certain limits, which are set by the vocabulary and habits of thought which he inherited or which he has learnt and adopted.

A way of life, inherited or freely adopted, or a combination of these two, causes a man to think of selected aspects and features of his future, which become focuses of his desire or aversion, and to be wholly uninterested in features that are strongly marked in the moral vocabulary attached to another way of life. The future, as he envisages it and as he describes it to himself in advance, thinking about it and discussing it with others, does not have all the interesting features which the actual future has, when it comes, for two reasons. First, the future which is present to a man's mind never exhausts all the features that might without absurdity be mentioned in moral claims and comments; the description is never an ideally complete description. The second reason is that the future always has a margin of uncertainty, of unknown contingencies, which were not expected and not intended. Expectations and intentions at any time purport to include only a few of the features which will be features of the future; more that is of moral interest will normally happen than could be either expected to happen or intended to happen. There is material for conflict of moral claims, for example, in the unexpected and unintended bad features of situations which had been envisaged as having predominantly good features; this on the objective side. On the subjective side there is material for conflict of moral claims in the experience of moral aspirations and emotions which do not converge on single objects, or single types of object; and the divergences are brought to the surface by common situations in which features judged good and bad are combined; and the divergence is particularly evident when the good and bad are combined unexpectedly, in a complex situation.

The conflict of moral claims arises from these two sides, subjective and objective, taken together. But it can be suppressed by an act of will binding the future and by a resolution that, as a matter of policy, superficially conflicting moral claims are to be settled by appeal to a single criterion. This is a decision to override the experienced conflicts for reasons taken to be of overriding moral and philosophical weight; philosophical, because they probably rest on an idea of rationality and of scientific method and on a rejection of unmethodical intuitions. Probably a theory of knowledge is invoked as support, one that dismisses the claims that I have made for the respectability of intuitions in this area. The decision to adopt a single criterion – for example, the greatest happiness or the least suffering or the greatest satisfaction of preferences – is made by modern utilitarians with an awareness that normal intuitions suggest a plurality of criteria, if criteria are invoked at all.

The variety of situations, and of morally relevant features of situations, is always unpredictable and uncontrollable, and therefore no rational man ought to be sure in advance of experience that his single criterion will not produce unacceptable results. This argument has force principally for someone who accepts the Aristotelian epistemology of moral judgement; namely, that intuitions of the rightness or wrongness of particular actions in particular situations are the principal, though not the sole, grounds upon which general aims and long-term policies rest, even though there is a reciprocal grounding of judgements of right and wrong in particular cases in considerations about general aims and long-term policies. The famous sentences on method in Book I of the Nicomachean Ethics say that thought on practical questions, whether prudential or moral, likewise in arts, crafts, skills, proceeds in an up-and-down way, from particular cases to general principles and back again from general principles to particular cases. But it must be admitted that there is no irresistible transcendental deduction which will prove that all practical thought must follow this pattern, if it is to be coherent. The utilitarian can argue that practical thinking in moral contexts is distinguished from practical thinking of all other kinds precisely by the single goal and by the simple criterion of right action, which are not to be found either in aesthetic contexts, or in any other kind of practical thinking. The man who claims to be sure that a single criterion must override all others for *a priori* reasons, in advance of all future experience, does not make an incoherent claim or an unintelligible one; nor does he commit himself to a policy which he cannot carry out in practice. A rebuttal, at once valid and persuasive, would need to suggest particular cases, actual and imaginable, which would illustrate the vast variety of possible situations of conflict between irreducible claims and goals, and which might cause him to doubt that his assurance of a single aim and simple policy coheres with his own thinking in particular cases. He may have failed to recognize the amount of forced simplification of difficult cases to which he is committed by the single criterion; and he may be deceived in his belief that no particular situation would ever disturb his *a priori* assurance about his overriding aim. He *may* be persuaded; but there is no absolute necessity that he should be, no final proof. Moral theory, like other practical theories, is not a matter for conclusive and irresistible demonstration. The superiority of one moral theory to another is established by showing that it gives a more simple and more comprehensive, and a less exception-ridden, account of the whole range of one's moral beliefs, and of the relation of one's moral beliefs to beliefs of other kinds, particularly philosophical beliefs. This is the Aristotelian theory of moral theory.

7

The checking of general moral theory against judgements about particular cases, and of judgements about particular cases against general moral theory, is a normal process of thought with which everyone is familiar. But there may be big differences in the emphasis placed upon the general as against the particular, and upon philosophical theory as against intuitions about particular cases. A Benthamite is gripped, like Bentham himself, by a philosophical theory that only one way of life is eligible by rational men who have got rid of those theological and moral superstitions, which suggest alternative ways of life other than the prudent pursuit of general welfare. He has philosophical beliefs about the requirements of rational methods of argument, and about the need to make moral issues determinate and clear, like the issues in an applied science. He probably believes, for instance, that the judgements which I have been calling intuitions are better assimilated to expressions of feelings and of emotional attitudes, which are natural in childhood and in pre-reflective societies, but which must be discarded by adults capable of systematic and scientific thought. The true utilitarian has the sense of unmasking and of penetrating behind pretences and superstitions and illusions to a single inborn and clear end of action which they conceal. He thinks that the superficially various virtues and various ends of actions are to be explained by reference either to utility or to surviving superstition, without remainder. If he is consistent in his utilitarian beliefs, and if he adjusts his particular judgements to his theory and acts accordingly, then he makes wrong judgements on occasion and in consequence acts wrongly: so I believe. Is this a mere confrontation between us without rational solution, or can the argument be pressed further? The suggestion that moral beliefs are not properly called beliefs is associated with the philosophical theory that very general differences of moral outlook are not accessible to further rational argument, beyond the stages of argument already mentioned.

8

The argument that might be pressed further is a philosophical one because it turns upon the relation of theory to practice quite generally. If the features of successive situations confronting us, which are relevant to our aims and interests, cannot be exhausted in our thought, and if we know this, then we are foreclosing, and restricting, thought if we cling to a single criterion of right action, and to one overriding aim, and if we exclude new considerations, and new features, from our attention. This will be true of every form of practice, whether it is a game, an applied art or craft, and the display and application of any kind of skill. There will always be a gap between the theory of good performance, necessarily stated in rather general terms, and the various details of actual good performances. The single criterion makes new, exploratory thinking on aims and ambitions redundant and unprofitable.

In *Thought and Action* (new edition, Chatto and Windus 1982) I stressed the inexhaustibility of features that may be discriminated within situations requiring action and that may be morally interesting, and of the confinement within a morality left to itself, not to be further developed imaginatively, as a giving up of much of practical thinking. There is some force of rational persuasion, and there is more than rhetorical force, in an argument from the curtailment of further thought and imagination, as an implied consequence of a policy, to the conclusion that that policy is wrong: at least in the sphere of morality, in a wide sense. Having the power to invent ways to think about differently characterized alternatives, and to weigh good and bad features of situations and of actions and of ways of life on several different scales, is one distinction of the species; it is one power that makes friends interesting to each other and that makes the species interesting to itself, and that makes its future interesting. The single criterion and single aim theories discard the peculiar interest of the species, and the interest of its future, as perpetually open to unforeseen alternatives through continuous thought. The single criterion arrests development, both historical and personal. The indefinite multiplication of satisfactions is a lesser prospect than the open possibility of the invention of new and unforeseeable ways of life.

This argument is not a transcendental argument, in Kant's sense, and it does not lead to a claim that its conclusion is a necessary one. But it is a properly philosophical argument from the phenomena of choice and of desire under alternative descriptions: an argument from the nature of intelligence in the species.

The argument runs: if the single criterion in ethics is accepted by someone, that person decides to restrict the peculiar powers of his intelligence and of his imagination; and he decides to try to set a final limit to the indefinite development of moral intelligence when he prescribes the single criterion to others. This is not a logically impossible conclusion; but it is an unconvincing one. The desires of human beings are desires for objectives represented in their thought under noble or agreeable descriptions, and men act under the pressure of these descriptions, seeing their actions as manifesting desirable dispositions and as being part of an admired, or loved, or sought after, way of life. Some large part of the value of their lives, as they see them and as their friends see them, resides in the imaginative thought that in this way informs their actions. A simplification of thought, and the possibility of clearly calculated solutions to moral problems, are often mentioned as reasons for accepting single criterion theories, and particularly these reasons are mentioned by utilitarians. But it is difficult, because unnatural, to discard the complexity of the thought by which we represent our dispositions and actions to ourselves, looking for better descriptions of them, and a better understanding of them; it is also an impoverishment, and a loss of the interest of experience and of attachment to the future. Utilitarian thinking is a kind of moral Esperanto. It forbids one to cross frontiers into a different country, to be a tourist or to emigrate, in thought. If a single criterion were accepted, the future becomes uninteresting – or at least less interesting, both for individuals, and for any particular society; and the future of mankind as a whole becomes less open. For such reasons as these a conflict of claims, which is not to be settled by a single overriding criterion, seems to be a necessity in our nature, and not just a superficial characteristic of practical thought at present, but an essential one, not to be eliminated.

9

Conflict of claims, which each seem binding, and which cannot both be satisfied in some individual case, has been most carefully studied in jurisprudence. The reasoning that balances contrary legal principles, contrary in the particular case, is a kind of exact reasoning, studied and refined for centuries. It exhibits the familiar, circular pattern of general principles being used to guide decision in particular complex cases, and particular cases being used to modify general principles and to suggest new ones. Secondly, legal reasoning recognizes the unpredictable variety of circumstances which leaves a margin of indeterminacy, an area for legal argument and for judicial discretion, when laws and legal principles are interpreted and applied. Imperfect fit between general principles and particular cases is assumed in the working of legal systems.

This resemblance between the practical reasoning of lawyers about the law and practical reasoning on matters of moral concern is imperfect. For instance, it is a normal requirement placed upon legal arguments, when a conflict of claims is being settled, that the principles and reasoning upon which the settlement has been decided should be clearly and fully stated; they must be available for reference and usable as precedents in subsequent arguments and decisions. This is a requirement of entire explicitness. There is no such requirement placed upon the settlement of conflicts of moral claims, not even when the conflicting moral claims are in the public domain and call for policy decisions. It is not necessary, although sometimes it may be useful, that a carefully drafted formula should be promulgated, when a significant moral decision is made, and that it should be available as a precedent. The continuity that links moral decisions, whether by a public body or by an individual, is a constant tendency to contribute towards a preferred way of life, with a constant order of priority among the human qualities sustained in that way of life. Even when moral argument centres upon principles and a conflict between them, the rational basis of the argument is rarely an appeal to precedent, and to the need to conform to precedents, but rather to the overall priorities in a way of life.

It is another aspect of the difference between a moral, and a merely legal, argument around a conflict of claims, that imagination will not be called for in legal argument as it often will be in moral contexts. Aristotle assimilates moral reasoning, and the balancing of conflicting principles in particular cases, to procedures in crafts and arts, and also in medicine, because there is the same necessity that rules, and the theory behind the activity also, should always be imprecise, rough and ragged at the edges, liable to exceptions, lacking in *ἀκϱίβεια*, which means accuracy in the sense of 'finish', as when a statue is unfinished because not polished, left in the rough, or when a drawing is left as a sketch. A trained judgement, together with some flair and a natural feeling for the subject-matter, enables the best performers to use the theory and principles of the craft, whatever it may be, up to the point at which they have to balance contrary principles and to find the right move without the guidance of principle.

This Aristotelian theory, which is a kind of epistemology of action, still has a useful application to ethics, in reminding one of how unexceptional moral judgements are, in spite of the suggestions of empiricist philosophers. 'You must not stress *rubato* passages in your playing: that is bad' and 'You must not invest all your money in one investment' are sentences which are grammatically, epistemologically, and logically, neither more nor less anomalous and exceptional than 'You must not allow your purely personal feelings to influence your verdict.' Nor are any of them anomalous and exceptional as utterances. Also there are good theoretical reasons in each case which could be quoted in their support. The principle stated for the piano serves an aesthetic ideal which in turn has an aesthetic theory behind it. Within the theory the vice of excessive *rubato* is an instance of a more general vice that corrupts music. The principle of divided risk is justified by the function of investment and is part of a modest theory of investment. The moral principle is justified as constitutive of the virtue of justice as fairness and of the ways of life of which fair verdicts are a part. Each injunction can be supported both by *a priori* arguments, and also by appeal to the experience and judgement of experienced practitioners. They may come into conflict, in exceptional circumstances, with other general principles which are equally well supported by theoretical arguments and by long experience of particular cases.

10

There are further reasons why practical reasoning on moral questions should occasionally lead to conflicts of principles, even apart from the conflicts that attend all practical reasoning, no matter what the subject-matter. Conflict of principles is overdetermined. Aristotle implied that moral questions are questions of finding the right balance among human interests, and he implied that each of the virtues, justice included, could be exercised to the full within a single complete life, and that there need be no final incompatibility between them. He claimed that, taking a man's life as a whole, there is no necessary incompatibility between the central virtues, all of which can be manifested in a complete life: though, he would add, only with luck. A man needs to have luck on his side if he is to realize the various ends that together constitute a desirable life. Aristotle claimed that there is no feature of human nature which entails that some virtues can only be attained at the expense of others in the long run, and the long run is a complete life: practical wisdom, for example, at the expense of theoretical understanding, or justice at the expense of friendship. Because of misfortunes, a man may in fact have to choose between friendship and justice, or to compromise between them. He will not usually be guided in the decision by any formula or test or clear criterion. He will have to make a judgement and to strike a balance guided by a conception of how the best form of life, taking his life as a whole, is to be realized. Each course of action perhaps has an evil aspect to it, and would be a blot on the record, a lapse from the conception of life as it ideally should be, even if an unavoidable lapse. The occurrence of conflict in particular cases depends on the uncontrolled and largely unpredictable turn of events in the external world, and in this sense on chance.

Let us assume that the dispositions towards justice and friendship are present in a particular man in an equal degree; he has these virtues, and he wants to be fair in making a particular award; but he also wants to avoid suffering, and he knows that he cannot, in the particular case, do both these things, because the man who on merit deserves to lose will suffer greatly and the man who will win will not be greatly pleased, nor would he suffer much if he lost. This happens not to be an occasion on which a satisfactory compromise can be made or a comfortable balance struck. I am assuming one has to lean towards one prohibition or the other, taking into account all the circumstances. Perhaps a just and truthful verdict has to be given in this case, in spite of the consequences. The balance may be struck, in the normal turn of events, in a complete life, in which both concerns, a concern for justice and also kindness, are liable to have their run: liable to, because a complete life itself depends on fortune and not on reason, and cannot be guaranteed.

Justice is in Aristotelian theory the central moral virtue, subordinated only to practical intelligence itself. A just man has sound intuitions and a trained feeling for avoiding partiality. This dependence upon intuition, and on perception of the just balance, is not a sufficient reason for classifying such judgements as neither correct nor incorrect. Flair is required, a sense of proportion, a capacity to hold in mind the different considerations, and not to be caught by outbursts of unconsidered emotion. Ross's book *The Right and the Good*, the original work of an Aristotelian scholar, was often dismissed in the 1930s and later as innocent self-parody, because Ross expounded his theory of *prima facie* duties and obligations, and of their typical conflicts, with a temperate tone and a judiciousness thought inappropriate to moral dilemmas; and he used banal and trivial examples. The contrast between the cloistered Aristotelian scholar, unaquainted with tragic situations and violent alternatives, and the existential moralist, who confronts impossible choices with a glowing authenticity, is facile and misleading. The difference is more one of style and of tone, than of logic and of substance, as can be seen if one takes the standard examples from a post-war existentialist writing.

In an occupied country a young man has to decide whether to join the resistance movement and thereby to bring punishments upon his family, who ask him to remain with them and to protect them. He recognizes both the claim of patriotic duty and loyalty and also the claim of loyalty to his family and the obligation to them which he knows that he has. Whatever his own set of moral beliefs, and whatever moral theory he accepts, if he theorizes at all, he would recognize that there are two apparent claims upon him. His own moral beliefs will determine both how he represents this apparent conflict to himself, and also how he argues with himself about them, if he is uncertain and if he needs to think carefully about them.

The valid point which an existentialist philosopher can make against Ross is that the conflict between *prima facie* duties and obligations, and the conflict of loyalties, in the example given constitute a conflict between two ways of life, and not merely a conflict between claims within a single way of life. There are extreme situations, not rare in this century, in which the subject reasonably sees himself as confronted with a choice between two different ways of life, which cannot be combined into one; and this great choice may be concentrated, and usually is concentrated, in a particular conflict of duties on a particular occasion, and it may never come up for consideration in an abstract way and as a general issue.

The notion of commitment has its place here. The young man is required to choose between the commitment to a life, or to a considerable part of a life, as a resister, as a member of a revolutionary movement, and as the servant of an overriding political cause, and on the other side the commitment to a life of decent usefulness and of family loyalty. The first commitment will demand the virtues of courage above all, of dedication, selflessness, also of loyalty; it will also call for violence, skill in deceit, readiness to kill, and probably also false friendship and occasional injustice. The second will demand the virtues of friendship and affection, gentleness, justice, loyalty, and honesty; it will also call for acquiescence in public injustice, some passivity in the face of the suffering of others, some lowering of generous enterprise and energy because of political repression. These are two different ways of life, because they demand different dispositions and habits of mind, different social settings, and different ends of action. The young man has to choose between two possible types of person, each with his own set of virtues and defects, now incompatible sets.

That conflicts of duties sometimes pose great choices of ways of life, as well as conflicts within a preferred way of life, is a valid objection to Ross, and perhaps to most moral philosophies described as intuitionist. Intuitionists usually argue from the assumptions that the *prima facie* duties themselves are not only immediately evident, but also are evident for reasons that cannot be further explained and expanded; and, secondly, that moral conflicts have to be settled without appeal to any further considerations external to the acknowledged duties themselves. Both assumptions are contrary to experience, and they go a long way to explain the usual hostility to intuitionism as a moral theory and to explain its implausibility. The theory employed the word 'intuition' to mark a full stop to reasoning, where there need be no full stop. We know that the specific moral claims, in conflict in a particular situation, often uncover also a conflict between two ways of life, both of which incorporate sets of virtues greatly sought after and admired by the subject. The particular situation becomes exemplary and focuses the larger conflict. The choice between the two ways of life, with their constitutive virtues and defects, is open to reflection and to discussion: which virtues are incompatible with each other, under present and foreseeable social conditions and in the light of what is known of psychology and of ordinary human experience, past and present? Are the repugnant features, different in each way of life, ineliminable? Is a commitment to one of the two irreversible? Are both ways of life likely to endure indefinitely, or does one of them, at least, depend on social and political conditions that are temporary? These are just a few of the questions that are likely to be relevant. There would not be an undiscussable issue, not amenable to argument about matters of fact and to arguments about desirable alternatives, leaving the subject blankly staring at stark alternatives with nothing more to be said.

There are certainly conflicts of duties, and of other moral claims, such as obligations, which do not bring into focus a conflict between ways of life. Within a single ideal of character and action, and within a single conception of priorities among sought after activities and interests, there must occasionally be an awkward impossibility of doing both of two equally necessary things; at least this must be so, if human interests, and the activities and traits of character and the sentiments to which men aspire, are not extremely simple, as utilitarians suggest that they are.

11

Existentialists argue against Aristotelian essentialists that an individual's act of commitment to a particular way of life is the reality which is camouflaged by the pretence of a single way of life as the one good for man deducible from his essential nature. Does not the recognition of commitment, and of occasions of great choice, entail the denial that there is anything that can properly be called the good for man? Are there not in reality, and as experience teaches us, many different ways of life, which are reasonably counted as possible ideals to be aimed at? Does not history provide examples of the contrasting ideals?

At this famous crux distinctions need to be made, and they are distinctions that are not clearly made by Aristotle and by those who turned his philosophy into dogma. 'The good for man' can be taken to mean the set of activities, and corresponding dispositions, which after reflection are most sought after and which after reflection are most admired and praised, together with an order of priority among these essential virtues. So interpreted, the good for man can be made, and should be made, the subject both of *a priori* argument and of *a posteriori* argument from history and from personal experience. Which are the most admired, the most noble and praiseworthy and desirable, human characteristics and activities, after reasonable argument and reflection? The arguments are always imprecise and inconclusive; but still there is a convergence upon a list of generally recognized and familiar human virtues, which are differently ranked and stressed at different times and in different places. Put together in one definite order, they can constitute one ideal way of life, a distinct ideal of perfection and completeness, one among others.

At this abstract level, the good for man, the moral ideal, is to be compared with the ideally healthy man, the medical and physical ideal, a similarly abstract conception, not without its usefulness. Plainly men have greatly varied in weight and stature and dietary needs and muscular development and in resistance to disease at different times and in different places. Teaching medicine, a doctor might still show a diagram, and give an account, of a normally healthy man and of his functioning, perhaps tacitly presupposing that the normal man is to live in the climate in which the lecturer and his audience are placed and to be faced with similar conditions. The account would still be very abstract, until he complicated the picture by showing the effects of urban stresses, pollution, sophisticated diets, sedentary habits, and so on, together with the virtues of the body desirable under these conditions, which would not be so desirable for men living in South Sea islands, largely unclothed and with a plentiful local food supply, and a relaxed, but highly regular, way of life. Similarly, the good for man, the abstract ideal, will step by step be made more concrete, and be brought nearer to actual moral problems, as the social and political and cultural conditions in which a man or woman must design their way of life are more closely specified.

There is a greater degree of freedom of choice, and a greater degree of indeterminateness, in arriving at the moral ideal than in arriving at the norm of good health, just because health is a subordinate end and an instrumental good and therefore it is open to a functional test; therefore with a subordinate good there is no place for the notion of commitment.

The only value of the analogy is that it explains the distinction between 'the good for man' as the name of an entirely abstract ideal, and the limited moral ideals between which a man in fact has to choose, and to one of which he commits himself, in an actual historical situation. The good for man, in the singular, is not one of the ways of life, specifically described and related to specific known conditions, which an individual has to choose or reject in a particular emergency. Rather it is the vaguely described target which he ought to choose to aim at, in preference to a life of pleasure, another possible target, and in preference to making fame and reputation his aim, and in preference to any other subordinate good taken from the set of good things which together constitute the good for man.

The correct answer to the old question – 'Why should it be assumed, or be argued, that there is just one good for man, just one way of life that is best?' – is an indirect one and it is not simple. One can coherently list all the ideally attainable virtues and achievements, and all the desirable features of a perfect human existence; and one might count this as precribing the good for man, the perfect realization of all that is desirable. But the best selection from this whole that could with luck be achieved in a particular historical situation by a particular person will be the supreme end for him, the ideal at which he should aim. It is obvious that supreme ends of this kind are immensely various and always will be various. There can be no single supreme end in this particularized sense, as both social orders and human capabilities change.

12

Sometimes the name 'ethical relativism' has been given to the doctrine that judgements about vice and virtue, right and wrong, and about the ends of action, cannot be 'objective', because, first, they evidently vary as social conditions vary and vary over a wide range: also because there is no way of showing conclusively, or by probable and plausible argument, that one of the very different historical ideals is to be preferred to the other. The ethical relativist argues that there is no Archimedean point, external to a particular local moral ideal, from which all the local moral ideals can be judged and evaluated. To take these points in reverse: the Aristotelian denies that there is no external and neutral standpoint from which the various historically conditioned moralities can be judged. Precisely the force of the Aristotelian good for man is that it does single out, in necessarily vague terms, the perfect life for a man, taking account of his unconditioned powers of mind; and that this abstract ideal constitutes the permanent standard or norm to which the historically conditioned moralities can be referred, when they are to be rationally assessed. In fact the historically conditioned moralities do converge upon a common core and are not so diverse as the relativists claim. Courage, justice, friendship, the power of thought and the exercise of intelligence, self-control, are dispositions that in the abstract ideal are the essential Aristotelian virtues, although the concrete forms that they take greatly vary in the different socially conditioned moralities. The virtues of splendid aristocratic warriors are not the same as the virtues of a Christian monk; but they are not merely different. Each of the two ways of life demands courage, fairness or justice, loyalty, love and friendship, intelligence and skill, and some self-control.

Every distinct way of life calls for these essential virtues, in one of their many versions and orders. They constitute the substance of morality, and the notion of virtue, and therefore of morality, are to be explained by reference to them. Relativism only becomes a plausible doctrine when it asserts that the particular forms which justice, courage, friendship, self-control, intelligence take will always greatly vary, as cultures and social structures vary. We can recognize different moralities as being all moralities, through the common core at an abstract level, just as we can recognize different codes of manners as all codes of manners, and different systems of law as all systems of law, in spite of the varieties of them.

To summarize: in many particular situations a balance has to be struck between the different virtues, and a balance has to be struck between the different interests and ambitions that are elements in the best current attainable way of life. This is not necessarily the kind of conflict which is intended when moral philosophers speak of tragic conflicts, irresoluble conflicts, and final conflicts; in the latter kinds of moral conflict the notion of striking a balance between conflicting virtues and conflicting duties, a balance that may prove to be the best one, when a whole life is considered, seems inappropriate. The difference between the two senses of conflict of duties and of virtues, or the two kinds of conflict, may be illustrated by the example mentioned above. The young man who has to choose between the resistance movement and the safety and happiness of his family does not have a choice, like that between generosity and prudence, which every normal man may expect to make from time to time, as one may expect to choose on occasion between justice and benevolence, or between fairness and friendship, or between truth and kindness; these may be called the normally unavoidable conflicts, requiring right judgement in the particular case and a balance between dispositions. The young man's conflict does not seem to involve finding the right balance between two elements of a single way of life; rather the choice can be seen as involving the abandonment of one way of life for another, although it need not be seen in this way.

One can call the end for man a single criterion, if one is prepared to speak of a criterion which is designed not to yield determinate answers. Do you have a criterion by which you can distinguish good food from bad, if you learn that good food has the right balance between contrasting flavours, and when you ask what the right balance is, you are told that it is the balance which the really discriminating cook-gastronome perceives in the particular case? I do not intend by this comparison to belittle or mock Aristotle's single, overarching end. On the contrary, I think the notion of balance represents a deep moral idea. The combining in the right proportions of political and purely intellectual concerns, of reason and emotion, of public and private activities, of justice and friendship, of prudence and spontaneity, is a carefully thought out ideal and part of the Greek tradition, and was founded on the belief that the soul, and the body also, have to be a balance of elements. That is how they, and other living systems, work, and 'unbalanced', whether of mind or body, is one step away from 'destroyed'.

But other moral theories stress another kind of conflict, not admitting of resolution by intuitively judged balance: a conflict between two purposes or policies either of which, if chosen, would destroy any balance between essential, but competing, concerns and would involve a drastic amputation either way: this is the existentialist case of the conflict between resistance to tyranny and loyalty to family in an extreme situation. As soon as one contrasts the two kinds of conflict, it becomes evident that the Aristotelian supreme end stands, as he intended that it should, on the borderline between being a meta-ethical claim and being a first-order moral idea. The notion of an overarching end, of a balance of virtues, may be rejected by a choice of a drastically specialized concern, or group of concerns, and therefore of an amputated existence, serving some entirely dominant interest; this has plainly been not only a romantic ideal, but a religious ideal also at various times. It seems to be the contrary of the Aristotelian good for man.

Can the argument between these apparent contraries be pressed any further? Consider the romantic ideal of the man of imagination who, as an artist, neglects every duty and obligation which could stand in the way of the claims of his art upon him. He gives an absolute priority to the virtues of the imagination and to originality and to the invention of new forms of expression. If he is Flaubert, he will have reasons, the result of long reflection, rehearsed for his own thought and explained to his friends, repeatedly and throughout his life, for this ordering of the virtues of imagination and originality and for this preferred way of life. If he is Flaubert, he will not dispute the established and essential virtues of moral character; on the contrary he will insist that they are essential to any sustained achievement in art, as they are in politics and in private life. But he will adapt and correct and restrict the ethical ideal to take account of his historical situation, as he sees it, and of the peculiarities of his own temperament and emotional needs, as he believes them to be. He will find his justification in an argument that art has taken over some of the former functions of religion, and also that the distortions of modern life can only be rendered tolerable by aesthetic experience and the free exercise of imagination. He will argue also that the virtues of the family and of citizenship are beyond his reach, except at a very low level, and that his own power of thought takes the form of literary imagination, not of practical care for humanity, and also not of scientific intelligence, which he also deeply admires. He therefore derives the choice of his rather eccentric way of life, that of the dedicated and solitary artist, from the common core of moral ideals by an argument from the historical situation and the needs of his time, and not by an arbitary choice. He argues that his potentialities are not unrestricted by his inborn abilities and desires, and that, in the actual circumstances, he has to make a harsh choice and to discard some good things in order to realize others; a softer compromise would lead to an inferior achievement, with the abstract ideal still taken as the constant criterion of achievement.

That there should be an abstract ethical ideal, the good for men in general, is not inconsistent with there being great diversity in preferred ways of life, even among men living at the same place at the same time. The good for man, as the common starting-point, marks an area within which arguments leading to divergent conclusions about moral priorities can be conducted. The conclusions are widely divergent, because they are determined by different subsidiary premisses. Practical and theoretical reason, cleverness, intelligence and wisdom, justice, friendship, temperance in relation to passions, courage, a repugnance in the fact of squalid or mean sentiments and actions; these are Aristotle's general and abstract terms, which do not by themselves distinguish a particular way of life, realizable in a particular historical situation. The forms that intelligence and friendship and love between persons, and that nobility of sentiment and motive, can take are at least as various as human cultures; and they are more various still, because within any one culture there will be varieties of individual temperament, providing distinct motives and priorities of interest, and also varieties of social groupings, restricting the choice of ways of life open to individuals.

In the light of this distinction between the abstract ideal, the good for man in a perfect life, and the relatively specific and limited way of life chosen by individuals at definite historical junctures, one may look again at the ancient question of the so-called objectivity of evaluations of ways of life, and of the virtues and the moral imperatives and the priorities which make up a way of life. The arguments around the abstract ideal, the perfection of men, are different in character from the arguments that lead a normally rational man to the choice of his particular way of life, or to his acceptance of the one that he finds himself born into and that he takes over without question. Arguments about the abstract ideal turn on the analysis of the notions of an end, on single or multiple criteria of rightness, on the notion of good, on the conflict of moral claims, and on what makes a context a moral one; in fact the arguments are those already deployed here. The arguments are largely philosophical and largely *a priori*, although they also mention very general features of common experience and of observed human nature.

The concept of morality, like the concepts of art or law or custom or religion, defines an area of argument which has not greatly changed for two thousand years; the same central notions recur in analysing this concept itself and the nature of virtue and in discussions of the possibility that pleasure constitutes the sole good. But the arguments that enter into the actual decisions, the crucial ones, which determine, step by step, a person's way of life and his moral character, invoke the particularities of his historical situation, his temperament, his beliefs, particularly his political and religious beliefs, and his natural abilities and education.

Conclusions about the abstract ethical ideal, the perfect good for man, are to a high degree objective, though not in the sense that the argument for one abstract ideal can be conclusive and may amount to a final proof that this must be the ideal: but objective, in the sense that the validity and relevance of the supporting arguments do not vary with the varying circumstances in which they are invoked, but are universal and independent of any particular standpoint or assumed premisses. Those utilitarians, who take pleasure to be the sole good and criterion of rightness, are committed to a set of implications which are as unavoidable today as they were when some of them were noted by Aristotle. There is very little looseness or freedom in the arguments in support of a single criterion propounded by the utilitarian and of multiple criteria propounded by the Aristotelian. The arguments converge upon a common pattern, and tend towards repetition, although it is always possible that new aspects of old arguments may be stressed, and even new arguments developed, by later philosophers.

On the other hand, the arguments that attach different priorities to different virtues, and that single out different moral imperatives as overriding, are uncontrollably various in varying historical situations and with the vastly varying circumstances in which individual agents may be placed. Even the word 'virtue' itself now has an archaic and unnatural ring, sounding like a translation from Greek or Latin.

The theories of society, and also the actual experience, on which moral arguments may draw, are not only vast, if one looks to history and to anthropology, but they are indefinitely open to the future. New forms of life are always to be expected, and the advance of knowledge and of technology continues, and new options are opened. No convergence is to be expected, and the more specific arguments cannot claim to lead to conclusions that are binding on all men at all times. This is the sense in which the arguments do not lead to judgements that can be called objective, while a judgement about the priorities among virtues in the perfect life can claim to be objective, even though it cannot be conclusively proved either by deduction or by experiment, nor by some combination of them. Hedonism is not a logically incoherent doctrine, if cautiously stated, but its wrongness is an objective wrongness, if, as I have argued, it is wrong. There is a sense in which the judgement that Shakespeare was a great writer is an objective judgement, even though it cannot be proved. There is also a sense in which a legal opinion – for example, the interpretation of a statute – may be objective, even though there is no proof of correctness, in the mathematical sense, and no experimental confirmation is to be expected.

In a difficult conflict of duties, in a case which amounts to a conflict between two ways of life, as when a man chooses between his obligation to his family and his duty to resist tyranny, the judgement of the right course will not be, and will not generally be taken to be, objective, in that sense. He who makes the decision, and commits himself to one moral priority, and to one principle, rather than to the other, is not necessarily making a decision, and entering into a commitment, which is either the wrong decision or alternatively fixes the priorities in an order which all men should observe at all times. The reasoning that supports his decision, if he reflects, will usually mention his character and his situation and the general circumstances of his time. Not only this: but he will probably recognize that his choice of a way of life is underdetermined by the arguments that support his decision. In any difficult case of trying to choose the lesser of two evils, he will find himself 'weighing imponderables', and balancing considerations which do not tilt unmistakably in one direction rather than another. He often would not wish to say that his decision on the right course is objectively right, in the sense that in making the decision he is at the same time claiming universal agreement for it. He has taken account of his own interests and abilities and limitations, and of his own situation and of his own past, and, in the light of these considerations, he has made his own commitment. His conclusion may be underdetermined by the supporting arguments in the sense in which an unobvious judicial decision in a difficult case may be underdetermined by the arguments; a contrary decision would have been arguable, not just plainly wrong. But the word 'commitment' carries a more positive implication; the implication is that he has himself recognized that his choice is underdetermined by the reasons that support it, and, secondly, that he accepts responsibility for the choice as being his and his alone, without the support of any external authority.

The abstract ethical ideal, the perfect and most desirable life for a man in ideal circumstances, has to be mentioned only when a moral argument has been pushed to its limits and to its philosophical foundations. It is mentioned when ultimate priorities are in question. Otherwise serious decisions in moral contexts are typically decisions between imperfect alternatives, made in comparative ignorance of the outcome and of many features of the real situation, by a man who is aware that he must discard one essential feature of a praiseworthy existence in order to obey some even more essential imperative. Moral philosophy has sometimes unjustly been accused of banality and emptiness and unreality, because it remains at an abstract level, and because it does not reproduce the typical strain and difficulty of choosing between two courses of action, each of which seems utterly incompatible with the ethical ideal and a manifest evil, and yet choice is in the circumstances unavoidable. There is the strain and difficulty of the necessary loss of an opportunity of happiness, or of justice, or of friendship, or of intellectual excitement, or of social reform, which has been chosen only to avoid a great loss. This also belongs to the essence of morality.

It is a strength of Aristotle's moral theory that he thinks of morality and social policy as parts of a single subject, within which social policy is the more important and larger concern. A second strength is the thoroughgoing naturalism of his approach to moral problems in the Nicomachean Ethics.

Moral injunctions are to be thought of as a protection against a warped character, monstrous ambitions, corrupt appetites, and stunted and inhuman sentiments. They are to be thought of as a protection of innately preferred activities and sentiments, which bring pleasure with them, and against inhuman and conflict-laden activities and sentiments, which bring unhappiness with them. There is no independent, and no transcendental, sanction of moral restraints, and no authority external to men's experience of the workings of their own nature. The experience of ease and enjoyment of a way of life, as opposed to frustration and suffering, makes the crucial test, and people will in fact be guided by this test, if they are not governed by perverse passions. As felt pain warns us of some wound or infection in the body, so suffering warns us of some wound or corruption in thought or feeling.

But Aristotle has repelled many by the implication in his theory that there is a fixity in human nature, and therefore in the virtues, which justifies the complacent thought that the ends of action are immutable and fully known once and for all. This is the tidiness, and the limitedness, which have often been found both unrealistic and also morally repugnant.

I will not deny that the reflexive nature of thought, and the liberation that may come from it, and the accelerating growth of the physical sciences, do carry implications for moral theory which could not be recognized by Aristotle.

13

There is no comparably clear and classical theory superior to Aristotle's in the power to explain the range of our ordinary moral intuitions. But there is the barrier of modernity; by which I mean that there have been changes, both in knowledge and in ways of life, which have the effect of making Aristotle's reconstruction of moral, and particularly of political, thought seem incorrigibly incomplete. The succinct phrase for the barrier, and for the missing element, is the concept of freedom, which is applied both in individual psychology and in politics. It is notorious that this is the notion, imprecise and unmanageable, on which the barrier is built. Slavery was not for Aristotle an evil, even less the principal evil. The notions of freedom and of liberation are not be found at the centre of Aristotle's ethics and philosophy of mind. There is no place here for the suggestion that supposedly free men are in a state of servitude, because of ignorance and of thoughtless emotions, and that they need to be liberated through philosophical conversion, which will overturn many of their common sense beliefs. The exercise of the crucial powers of mind, of real intelligence and imaginative feeling, is not represented as a liberation from a natural state in which these faculties are blocked and not available. Nature and freedom are not in opposition. In a reasonably favourable social environment a character and moral temperament of the right kind will develop naturally by habituation. Similarly, his political thought does not have a place for freedom of individual choice as a value on the same level as justice in social arrangements; nor for respect for independence as a ground for action alongside respect for duties and obligations. His philosophy is, as it were, pre-lapsarian; neither in his philosophy of mind nor in his ethics is there some imagined redemption, or salvation, following upon a fallen state, a state of bondage.

A third aspect of the concept of freedom is missing, a third feature of a modern consciousness: the idea that all natural phenomena, including changes within the souls of men, are to be explained as instances of natural laws, and that nature is entirely uniform in the regular correlations of causes and effects: that there is a philosophical problem surrounding the idea of the morally responsible agent who has his own character to make and who is free to choose between good and evil; for it seems that his character directly, and his choices indirectly, must be the effects of innate and environmental conditions combined, and that he cannot be ultimately responsible for them, although he ought to be responsible for them.

The starting-point of ethics, as a philosophical inquiry, is changed by the three-sided concept of freedom, and so also are first-order moral anxieties, both political and personal. The philosophy of ethics in modern times begins with some account of the relation between the scientific point of view and the moral point of view towards conduct and character. As this relation is explored, the difference between a man's knowledge of his own actions and purposes and his knowledge of other people's actions and purposes is investigated also. Spinoza stands at the barrier of modernity on the modern side, preoccupied with all three connected aspects of the concept of freedom – liberation from the passions, freedom in society, and freedom in relation to the common order of nature, or, in short, metaphysical freedom.

14

When I first read Spinoza's *Ethics*, I was overwhelmed, as many others have been, by the fact that he was at once a moralist, writing from the moral point of view, and that he was also writing from the point of view of an imagined psychological and physical theory, deduced, as he thought, from first principles. He had not followed Aristotle in accepting the actual limits of human knowledge, as they were in his time. He made the assumption that no limit can be set to the development of systematic natural knowledge, and that a valid moral ideal must be compatible with the imagined future development of natural knowledge: more than compatible: that the enjoyment of such knowledge, and the desire to have the understanding that it brings, is a principal part of a reasonable man's ambition, and therefore of the moral ideal. Secondly, Spinoza considered the individual organism, which has to be both a receptacle of knowledge and an agent in pursuit of it, in an entirely naturalistic way, without ascribing to a person any unexplained or supernatural powers, or any powers that are not to be understood as a complication of the powers of living creatures generally. Therefore moral enlightenment, and the improvement of men and of society, have to be the effects of understood and controlled causes in the natural order of things. In so far as radical improvement is attainable, it is attainable in much the same way that an improvement in men's physical condition may be attainable, by the application of a more systematic knowledge of causes: both of causes operating in society, as indicated in Spinoza's two political works, and also causes operating in the individual.

We are now in a rather better position to interpret Spinoza's account of personality, and of the mind–body relation, than previous generations have been, partly because we have machine models of the mind, or of some features of the mind, and partly because materialist conceptions of the mind are now advocated and disputed among philosophers with more care than ever before.

Spinoza's theory of the mind has at the least the following sources: first, the Epicurean tradition, which requires that the separable soul or spirit, subject of speculation and myth in the established religions, should be shown to be without function and non-existent. This tradition required that pleasure and peace of mind should be the goals of moral concern rather than a standard of perfection established by *a priori* argument. Secondly, he rejected Descartes' theory of the soul as being like a pilot in a ship and argued that the person as a thinking being and the person as an extended thing must not be related externally, as in Descartes' theory; neither was merely an instrument in relation to the other, and neither had an absolute primacy. The difficulty and inconsistencies in Descartes' theory had shown Spinoza that the subject both of thought and of physical movements must be a person, and not in the one case a mind and in the other a body; and yet it is certainly true that thoughts can only be adequately explained by thoughts and motions by motions, as Descartes had argued. From Descartes also Spinoza takes the programme of reclaiming humanity from superstition and ignorance by a methodical correction of the intellect. But the method is different in Spinoza because there is no place for sovereign acts of will. The improvement is to come through the recognition and constant awareness of the difference between clear and connected thought and mere confusion of mind, and from the natural and innate desire of a person to be as free and self-determining as he is able to be.

The third source of Spinoza's theory of the mind is the new scientific enlightenment of his time, particularly the new physics, and, more specifically, optics, with which he was closely concerned. I cannot prove from biographical sources that he had thought continuously about the physical basis of perception, and particularly of sight, and that this thought had been the inspiration that led to his theory of mind and to his theory of knowledge; and that he thought about the nature of light and studied perspective and the corrections that the eye and brain make to the inputs received. But I am convinced that I can infer this from the nature of the theory itself together with the few known facts of his life.

When an adult human being, a child still in infancy, and an intelligent animal perceive an approaching object, or a distant object, there is a physical input in each case and a physical interaction also. The physical effects are very similar in all three cases, different only in so far as the eye, nervous system, and brain are different; the animal's brain and optical equipment are different from the human ones, and are apt to react to smaller ranges of differences of input. Like the adult, the infant and the animal react to the object with discrimination, and within limits intelligently, even though the thought that informs their behaviour is in neither case the conscious thought that is formulated in speech, or that could be so formulated. The motions in eye, nerves, and brain, in interaction with the environment, are to be explained within physics and without reference to any causes other than physical causes; and so also are the physical movements that constitute an element in the creature's behaviour. But the thought of the object seen as being of a certain kind, whether unconscious or conscious, unformulated or formulated, can only be explained by the thoughts that constitute reasons for further thoughts; and similarly also the thought that informs the behaviour is to be explained only by antecedent thoughts.

The thinking of adult human beings is of a complexity that allows thought about the causes that constitute reasons for their particular beliefs in a particular case. It allows also the further reflection on the goodness and badness of the reasons, as determined by an inborn standard of adequate thinking. So a person's perceptions, considered as thoughts, are indefinitely open to his corrections. The physical, bodily equivalent of this mental complexity is that complexity of the human brain which stores the effects of past inputs and which enables the new inputs to be combined with the traces of the old. Spinoza's speculation is that the material equivalent of the comparative autonomy of the rational, thinking person is the comparative independence of the physical structure which is the vehicle or instrument of thought, in the sense in which the eye is the vehicle or instrument of vision. The internal complexity of the human brain gives it a greater independence in relation to external influences. The traces of past inputs within the brain are linked and cross-linked in a vastly elaborate network; and this physical complexity is the material equivalent of the many-channelled capacity to learn and to acquire a variety of skills which distinguishes human thought from the less complex, and therefore more predictable, capacities of other animals. The human mind is relatively independent correspondingly. The thought that informs human behaviour and speech is not confined to routine reactions to the observed environment; it can proceed with some degree of autonomy, drawing on a vast store both of memory and of innate principles of reasoning.

The main subject-matter of morality is pleasure and pain, and the emotions, and the conversion of the emotions into forms of active and positive enjoyment. The emotions are thoughts about external things acccompanied by affect; they are ways of perceiving reality with pleasure or suffering. A jealous person is one with a belief about the causes of his suffering who traces the pain in his thought, whether conscious or unconscious thought, to a certain pattern of causes; he is therefore inclined to act against these causes. Just as a person corrects his first impulsive judgements of perception by reflecting on his limited evidence and point of view, so a person corrects his thoughts about the causes of his affects by reflecting on the inadequacy of these causal beliefs, and therefore on the inadequacy of his classifications of his own states of mind. Just as we come to realize that the systematic investigations of physics will reveal a different structure in the physical world from the structure of commonsense belief, derived from our perceptions of medium-sized objects: so a more systematic understanding of the connection of thoughts will show that our ordinary emotions, sentiments, and attitudes do not have the comparatively simple sources which we ordinarily suppose them to have.

15

There is one immense difference between ethics, which requires the correction of the intellect and the control of the passions, and medicine, the science that studies the strengthening of the body against disease. The correction of the intellect is an operation of thought upon itself. The instrument, and the material to which the instrument is applied, are of the same material. Doctors use physical agents as means to physical effects, and the laws of physics and of chemistry are necessary and sufficient to explain the physical changes that constitute a cure. The thought that informs the doctors' actions can be explained only by the thoughts, principally beliefs and desires, which the doctors have; and the relevant beliefs include beliefs about the laws of physics together with beliefs about the particular physical states of his patients or of himself, if he is his own patient. The moralist, correcting the mind and not the body, is a different type of agent, as is particularly evident when he is also his own patient, as he normally is. Then the thought of the need of a correction already amounts to a correction, or to the beginning of one. When a correcting thought is presented by a moralist to another person, as it were, to his patient, the thought, if understood, has an immediate effect on the thinking of the hearer.

The conduct of men is governed by their emotions. Their emotions are constituted in part by their beliefs about the causes of their pains and pleasures. These thoughts about causes have their own causes in other thoughts, and all thoughts can be made the subject of other thoughts. If I think about the state of my body and of the causes of that state, there is no immediate change in the state of body, or in the state of mind, as an effect of the mere fact that I have thought about them. But my thought about the approaching object in my line of sight, and my jealous thoughts about my neighbour, are immediately changed if I start to reflect on my thinking that the approaching object is a so-and-so and on why I think this, and if I reflect on why I think jealously about the man. The original thoughts are changed, just because the new thought about reasons, even if it confirms the original thought, still adds new reasoning to it; now my reasons are more articulated than they originally were, and in this sense also they have changed.

To take an example from judgements of perception, which I believe were for Spinoza the crucial case, illustrating the thought–body relation: I think an approaching object is a hornet, and then I reflect on why I think this, and I decide that it is the size of the creature and its colour that make me think this and reasonably make me think this. Reflecting on the reason has confirmed the original thought; but the original thought has been added to and complicated by the further thought that the connection between reason and conclusion is for further reasons sustainable. The structure has become more elaborate. This argument ought not to rest on a principle of individuation for thoughts, as if thoughts were like pictures or 'lifeless images', which could be counted. Spinoza explicitly rejects this conception of thinking, which is to be represented as a more or less continuous activity, and not as a succession of distinct thoughts.

The thinking of a person with a knowledge of astronomy when he looks at the setting sun, and thinks of it as setting, is very different from the thinking of the simple peasant who sees the same thing and who in a sense makes the same judgement. The sun is associated in the astronomer's thought with an extensive theory and not with a few unsystematized pieces of knowledge of external objects. He understands, in the light of theory, his own tendency to think of the sun as a comparatively small object suspended in the sky. He knows what makes him have this idea and why it is inadequate. He still has the same vision of the sun in the sky as the ignorant man. But this idea of the sun is surrounded in his thinking with thoughts that explain it, and, by explaining, correct it. Similarly, the jealous person, who has acquired a deeper understanding of his suffering, may find that jealous thoughts still occur to him. But he will in his own thinking modify these jealous thoughts with the fuller explanations that surround them. The passions and negative emotions of men rest, intellectually, upon an error of egocentricity and of short-sightedness. One sees the universe as revolving around oneself and one's own interests as central in it; and one cannot see past the immediate environment to the vast chain of causes that have led to the frustration of one's own desires.

Like the geocentric perceiver of the sun, one ordinarily has a false perspective and a false scale, and one's emotions betray this.

Spinoza's *Ethics* gives an account of a possible moral conversion which takes the form of an intellectual enlightenment acting on the emotions, which is not unlike a religious conversion. The language of salvation and beatitude that he uses enforces the analogy, a shaking off of the burden of illusion and anxiety; there is an echo of Lucretius. The enlightenment entails a change of standpoint and therefore a change of perspective; this is the parallel with the correction of perceptual judgements. A self-centred standpoint, determining a particular limited point of view, is to be succeeded by an attempt to understand one's own beliefs, sentiments, and attitudes from a more objective, less confined, point of view – ideally, from the standpoint of impersonal reason: at the least from a standpoint from which it is possible to examine the chain of causes which led to the original beliefs, sentiments and attitudes. An observer of physical objects corrects his judgements to take account of his particular position in the world. The correction of the emotions is an analogous process of putting the painter of the picture into the picture, and of thereby making the original picture a feature of the scene alongside the objects that it depicts.

Scholars writing about Vermeer remark on this favourite theme of that time, particularly in Holland, of reflections within a picture; on the fascination with the refractions of light and with optics, with Leeuwenhoek's microscope, and with the grinding of lenses and with mirrors. Admittedly the picture of the painter, or the reflection of him, within the painting is a device of mannerist style, and one must not over-stress the analogy. But the parallel between correction for point of view in perception, and correction by understanding of causes of sentiments, is plainly there in Spinoza. He takes perceptual knowledge, and particularly the double involvement of mind and body in the acquisition of it, as the starting-point for his account of knowledge of all kinds and of thought of all kinds.

An emotion has an object, and is a way of perceiving the world painfully or agreeably. It is an interaction with external objects, as vision and touching are. But the interaction in the case of emotion entails not only pleasure and pain but also the desire to pursue or to avoid. Nothing prevents the emotional subject from stepping back to put his own jealous thoughts, with their accompanying pain, into their proper causal setting, except the strength of the passion, and the lack of reflection and knowledge of causes. The jealous thoughts are undermined by a wider, reflective view of causes; they are undermined in the sense that the subject no longer believes them. They may linger on as impressions, as my impression of the sun as a small object in the sky lingers when I no longer believe that this is its nature. The original and persisting thought may be described as bracketed, or cancelled, by being put into relation with a more comprehensive and coherent set of beliefs.

It is the characteristic of men's thought that it is reflexive and that the activity of thinking entails a process of stepping back, in order to attain greater objectivity, by making corrections for point of view. Active conscious thought in men naturally turns into self-consciousness, into thought about thought. This is the respect in which thoughtful creatures are, or may be, comparatively autonomous: comparatively, but in no absolute sense. Human beings act from the desires which their emotions engender, and which are constitutive elements of their emotions. Their passive emotions are the effects of external causes acting upon their drive to self-preservation and to power through their conceptions, usually inadequate, of the external objects that are affecting them. People will behave more reasonably, and the social order will be improved, if and only if at least a ruling minority of persons are converted from egocentricity to detachment in their thought about themselves and about their relations to external things and persons. This conversion depends upon their realizing that their innate drive to increase their power and liberty requires disciplined thought, and an assertion of independence; this is a necessary but not a sufficient condition of the conversion. There may be emotional distractions that will stand in the way of clear and detached thought. Once a person realizes the power of thought, and exercises this power, he begins to enjoy the exercise and to feel the power of understanding, which is a positive pleasure, as people enjoy the exercise of physical powers. The drive for clear thinking and for understanding necessarily brings with it some self-knowledge and some degree of detachment from unconsidered and destructive passions; and this moral improvement cannot be achieved by any other means.

16

Spinoza's morality has as its terms of evaluation freedom of mind and independence, which are to be contrasted with confusion, obsession, and inner conflict. The ideal path of moral improvement leads from a state of being mentally confused, frustrated, and in a state of conflict to a state of being reasonable, clear-sighted, and at peace. The external manifestations of these states of mind will be hatred and conflict with other people on the one side and peaceful and friendly relations with other people on the other. The prohibitions and injunctions of conventional liberal morality, the *prima facie* duties, can be explained in two complementary ways; first, as being the prohibitions and injunctions that would naturally be respected by a liberated person, who would naturally want, for the sake of his own peace of mind, to behave as they prescribe and to follow the way of life which they protect. He would take pleasure in social harmony and friendship rather than in conflict and hatred. Secondly, the prohibitions and injunctions can be explained as the necessary protection of a social order that is indispensable to the free person's preferred way of life: reasonably peaceful and harmonious, reasonably tolerant, and free from either social conflict or tyranny.

Not all the conventionally accepted moral prohibitions and injunctions survive this double scheme of explanation. Some are only to be explained as consequences of superstitions and false philosophies, and cannot be explained as necessary protections of the way of life and of the social order which a free, intelligent person needs. Nor can they be explained as being principles of behaviour which an intelligent person will be naturally inclined to follow. They are therefore to be rejected. Most of them prescribe some form of asceticism, of renunciation of enjoyment without offsetting advantage, or they are tied to notions of sin and repentance, which in turn presuppose a personal God and divine judge, which are illusions, projections of human passions.

Sustained pleasure is the mark of virtuous activity, together with attachment to a community of persons sharing an overriding interest in thought and knowledge. Hatred and aggression, manifestations of divided and fluctuating impulses, are marks of vice, because they lead to destruction and suffering and are incompatible with freedom of mind and with free inquiry and an interest in truth and in theory. Hatred causes an answering hatred; for Spinoza the principal problem of politics is the breaking of such reinforcing circles of hostility, which will always arise from the uncontrolled emotions of the mass of people who are still incapable of critical reflection.

One cannot stress too strongly that for Spinoza virtue is its own reward and that the word does not have its usual Christian association with renunciation of selfish interests in his thought. An admirable person, described in the last part of the *Ethics*, enjoys his own energy and the exercise of his powers of mind, and he steadfastly protects himself against the normal suffering of the world and against the loss of his independence. He participates in every effort to protect and extend freedom of thought, and his own happiness and way of life depend upon it.

17

Spinoza's doctrine makes morality, in the ordinary sense of the word a means to, and a by-product of, liberation from obsessions and from prejudice and an emotional enlightenment; and this doctrine entails a different relation between the philosophy of morality and morality itself: different, that is, from that which I have attributed to Aristotle. Let me use the phrase 'rational reconstruction' neutrally and say that both philosophers offer a rational reconstruction of the first-order moral judgements generally accepted within the social groups to which they belonged. Spinoza makes a clear separation between the reasons with which the conventional moralist explains his moral prohibitions and the reasons with which the philosopher would explain the same prohibitions. Asked why fairness is always necessary, and why the law is usually to be obeyed, and why incest is wrong, the philosophical moralist will look for an explanation within the double scheme already described: first, what the reasonably liberated person wants and needs, and, secondly, what arrangements are necessary to preserve that kind of social order and way of life which the person with an inquiring mind needs. Considerations of these two kinds will cause the philosophically enlightened person to accept most of the prohibitions of western liberal morality as reasonable, and will lead him also to cultivate most of the virtues which are ordinarily accounted virtues by just, peaceful, and tolerant people.

Spinoza does not anticipate Hegel's 'the cunning of reason' as a concept; but he certainly thought that the drive to self-preservation, and hence to a necessary modicum of social harmony, has led us by experience to respect the usual set of necessary prohibitions and to admire the usual set of necessary virtues. But people are also ordinarily myth-makers and imaginatively superstitious, and they have needed supernatural beliefs as props to moral restraint. The myth of God's judgements and God's punishments serve to sustain moral prohibitions which can also be explained as dictates of reason.

Spinoza's theory of personality entails a revision of moral theory and entails that the intuitions of the majority have no peculiar and final authority as they have in Aristotle's philosophy. Aristotle gives authority to moral intuitions because they are the unreasoned expressions of desires and needs implanted in essential human nature. Spinoza did not think of ordinary moral intuitions as expressions of a human essence; within his metaphysics there is no such thing. The rational justification of those intuitions which can be justified is found in their utility. They usefully prescribe, for the wrong reasons, the conduct which the free person follows for his own adequate reasons, which are quite different from the reasons of the unphilosophical person.

That every person pursues the extension of his own power and freedom to its furthest limit is not ordinarily recognized and acknowledged, although a reflective person may bring into consciousness this central drive for power and freedom. Rather the drive, or conatus, is postulated as part of a very general theory of individuality, which applies not only to human beings, but to creatures of all kinds; and the drive is particularly conspicuous in all living organisms. It is a natural necessity that our desires should be so organized that they tend to our own preservation, and to the extension of our power and freedom, as we conceive them, though this tendency will be disguised by the confusions of thought that normally inform our specific desires. The specific desires that move a particular person to action at a particular time are the effects of causes which operate in accordance with the discoverable laws of thought. The association of thoughts, the ways in which they combine to form sequences, are no less regular and intelligible processes than the processes of physical change in the body and brain. Spinoza held that it would be as much an offence against reason to question the law of causality in the psychological domain as in the physical; but the causality that links thoughts to thoughts has a different form from the causality that links one physical change to another. Conflict of mind and mental agitation are the normal conditions of people, and war and civil discord the normal external conditions of their lives. Although there are good reasons why it is so, and entirely adequate explanations of this condition, it is also true that it need not always be so. How is this possible? Is Spinoza's psycho–physical determinism compatible with the call for emotional conversion and liberation from conflict by an enlightened enjoyment of intelligence and freedom of mind?

The answer is to be found in the nature of thought: specifically in the reflexiveness of thought, in the capacity to form ideas of ideas of ideas indefinitely: in the intrinsic characteristic of thought to be self-correcting, when thinking reaches a first stage of complexity, as it does in adult men. The attainment of a degree of complexity in thought is inseparable from, and is an expression of, the same degree of complexity of associated physical structure. At a very low level of complexity physical processes in the creature are intelligible as functions of the inputs interacting with a more or less constant internal structure. But when the percipient reviews and questions the perception, wondering whether it is to be endorsed as true, he is actively thinking; and the process of thought has its causes within itself and is less externally determined.

The needed injunction, therefore, the first commandment of a moralist, is the order actively to exercise the power of reflection, and to question immediate beliefs and sentiments. There should be a process of unmasking, of looking through the immediate classification of one's own attitudes and feelings to the more full, but disguised, connections of thought, which are the reality behind the appearances. That which a person believes about his own sentiments and desires in part determines what they actually are. So psychic appearances and the psychic reality are never to be entirely separated. No other appeal except the appeal to reflection is relevant; the passions, and the impulses which are part of them, are not to be controlled by the will, which is a fiction, but only by the self-altering activity of thought.

A person is free to change his moral opinions, and the emotions of which they are part, in so far as a change in them is not to be explained by a cause external to his own thinking, but is due principally to his own critical reflection, as far back as one can trace causes. The difference is one of degree, because no one's activity can be wholly independent of external causes. The activity of connected thought is the only activity of a person which may be autonomous and self-caused, in part and for limited periods. The chain of his thinking may at any time be interrupted by an emotionally charged association of ideas, which is unconnected with the previous order of his thoughts. The power to think actively comes up against such limits continuously; but the power is always present in a sane and undamaged person.

The circuits of the brain function in accordance with the laws of physics, as do the sense organs and limbs and the human body as a whole. The ideas, which are ideas reflecting these bodily states, succeed each other in accordance with the laws of thought. The linkages are the linkages of ideas and these are regular and intelligible as sequences of thought, no less intelligible than the order of firing of neurons in the brain as a physical pattern. Spinoza notoriously claims that the order of causes is the same under the two attributes, in a sense of 'the same' which is not clarified. From the standpoint of the thinker, one can think of using one's brain, in the activity of thought, as one uses one's eye to see, or one's finger to feel. But one must not imply that a thought makes a physical configuration what it is, or that a physical configuration makes a thought what it is. Thoughts are only adequately explained by thoughts, and physical forces and configurations by physical forces and configurations. There are two utterly distinct, but indispensable, schemes of explanation with a common subject-matter, which is the total activities and reactions of human beings.

18

The freedom, which is the subject of Part IV of the *Ethics*, is the freedom that is conditional upon a degree of detachment both from the passions and from supernatural beliefs and fears: a familiar, Epicurean sense of freedom. But the background to it, the scientific determinism and the distinctive mind–body theory, lend the moral doctrine a new depth and weight of argument. From the standpoint of a rational, scientifically-trained, detached observer, one can view all human beings in two ways: biologically and physically as organisms, whose movements and responses, described in the terms of physics, illustrate the laws of physics: secondly, and equally, as thinkers whose beliefs, questionings, desires, emotions, illustrate intelligible connections of thought. The standpoint of the solitary Cartesian thinking subject is that of a man questioning the reasonableness of his own thought and of the desires and emotions formed by his thought. He then appears to himself as a creature who is partly dependent on the action of causes external to himself, limiting his freedom of action: and partly as a thinking subject, who, surveying his desires, beliefs, and emotions and their causes, may rearrange them, and their interconnections, with some independence of the external causes which originally made them what they are.

As a Cartesian subject, he can step back from his moral beliefs and his desires which he sees to be in part determined, for instance, by social and family influences; and he can test their validity by reference to an inbuilt standard, which is his own tendency to rational coherence and consistency in thinking. The balance or see-saw between self-determination and external determination is the form in which moral experience presents itself: a swaying balance between consciousness of oneself as agent and as patient, a natural object, as a link in a chain of causes. This polarity is the real basis, correctly understood, of the distinction between virtue and vice, good and evil. Moral good and evil, as ordinarily recognized, are deduced from freedom of mind and slavery to the destructive passions. A political philosophy is similarly deduced from this metaphysical distinction. But one may object that the question still not answered is – how is the perception of a person, from the standpoint of an external, scientific observer, to be reconciled with that same person's perception of himself as partly self-determined, partly not? It seems that there must be a conflict between the two perceptions of the same object. The external, scientific observer sees an undivided illustration of effects following from causes and of natural law, while the subject, reflecting on himself, perceives an all-important discontinuity between his phases of active thought and his passive emotions and imaginations, externally determined.

The conflict, which is not a contradiction, might be expressed in this way: from the standpoint of the individual the glimpses, and sudden experiences, of comparative freedom of mind and clarity of understanding are the supremely important experiences, moments of pleasure, fulfilment, illumination. From the standpoint of a scientific observer the fact that the process of thought is sometimes, and to some degree, a self-contained one, rational in form, while usually it is not so, is less significant. The connections and linkages of ideas in non-rational, and in irrational, thinking are no less susceptible of explanation, and may be no less interesting to the observer, than the linkages that constitute a standard form of argument. An observer who is not merely curious and merely scientific in his interests, but who is judging and evaluating the person observed, will make other distinctions. He will be interested in the balance between self-determination in a person's thought and his mere responses to external causes, and in the degree to which a person is an active, rational thinker rather than someone who is governed by obsessions and by unchecked fantasies and irrational hatreds. An observer will need to make this kind of judgement if he wishes to change the beliefs or desires of the person observed. Spinoza remarks more than once in his two political works that one needs, for political purposes, to notice the difference between people who can be persuaded to be reasonable by argument and people who must be moved by less rational appeals to the imagination and to emotions.

Men normally recognize that most of their beliefs and desires were originally the outcome of causes outside their own thinking. But their thought takes the form of a review of their beliefs and desires; they have the means, in language, to ask why they believe and desire what they do. Moral philosophy reinforces this asking of 'why?' and tries by its systematic arguments to make the reader more especially conscious of the standards of rationality which he is applying. Viewed from the standpoint of an observer, both his successes and failures, his periods of lucidity and his yielding to destructive passions, must have their explanation, even if the explanations are not known.

The contrast between the standpoint of the thinking subject, conscious of his own power to question his own desires, and the standpoint of the observer, seeking explanations of his changes of mind, is not to be found in Spinoza. Nor is the related contrast between the moralist, who prescribes and explains the best way of life and the virtues, and the scientist who discovers the causes that explain the actual virtues and vices of men in any particular case. This is a Kantian and post-Kantian contrast. I have added it as a gloss upon the notorious contrast within Spinoza's writing between the exhortation to correct the intellect and the simultaneous exhortation to abandon the dangerous superstitions that are associated with notions of free will. It is evident that for him these two exhortations are not only not in conflict with each other, but they are two connected, reinforcing parts of a single doctrine. Clearing one's mind of confusions and superstitious fears will always involve getting rid of the idea of oneself as an original cause and as a sovereign will and as an island in nature. The moments and phases of freedom of mind, which constitute a natural happiness, are moments when one is identified through one's own thought with the rational order of things. These are unegotistical moments, which bring satisfaction, excitement, and an elevation of mind, from two sources; first, the object of one's attention is intrinsically inspiring and sublime, and, secondly, one loses, in such phases of one's life, the sense of being narrowly confined within one's environment and of more or less helplessly reacting to it. There is a sense of power and of movement, and also of escape into the open and away from triviality, when one's thought moves into this larger natural element, which is the rational order of things, as revealed in physics and mathematics and in philosophy.

19

At this point I expect someone to press the following complaint: 'This may be a correct exposition of Spinoza, with some acknowledged modifications to fill a gap in his theory of knowledge: it is an exposition of a powerful and familiar set of moral attitudes, which contains a reverent, almost mystical, attitude to nature, and which traces cruelty and evil to their roots in inner conflict and which thinks of virtue as sanity and enjoyment of living and of vice as mental derangement. This is all very well', the objector continues, 'but what reasons can be given for accepting

Spinoza's moral theory? Do you finally accept Spinoza's drastic reform of our moral intuitions rather than Aristotle's rational reconstruction of the reasoning that lies behind our standard moral intuitions?' I am inclined to think that Spinoza comes nearer to an acceptable position.

There are two principal reasons that influence me: the first is his theory of the mind and of personality, the so-called double aspect theory of personality, which insists that thoughts explain thoughts, and physical changes explain physical changes. The second reason is his consistent naturalism, and the theory of knowledge that goes with it. I shall consider them in order.

Spinoza's moral theory, which shows the path from mental servitude to enlightenment, is itself derived from the theory of the two attributes, thought and extension, under which a person's activities and states can be described and explained. This obscure theory about the mind–body relation, and of how it must be understood by us, seems to me plausible, and my reasons for thinking this are independent of morality and of moral theory. If the double aspect theory of the mind–body relation at least is plausible, then some of our established ways of speaking about persons' abilities and powers and dispositions and emotions need to be reconsidered.

The double aspect theory of personality may be summarized as follows:

(a) As we see with our eyes, so we think with our brains, and eyes and brain pass from one state to another in accordance with the laws experimentally established in physics as laws of motion which are universally valid.

(b) All creatures think, and their behaviour can be described, both in physical terms, in terms of movement, and in mental terms, that is, in terms of what they want and of what they think about their environment. Human beings are exceptionally complex organisms, and are comparatively so much more self-determining and so much less determined by the immediate environment, that their desires and beliefs rise to the level of conscious desires and beliefs. Consciousness entails reflection and self-correction. It remains true that they can represent their behaviour to themselves as physical events and movements and also as the outcomes of desires and beliefs.

(c) Thoughts, including desires and beliefs, can only be adequately explained by connections natural to thought, as physical movements and changes can only be adequately explained as the effects of other physical movements and changes. We may observe, and rely on, correlations between physical changes and changes in belief and thought and, even more obviously, there are changes in our thoughts which are followed by physical changes. But there can be no systematic, theoretical understanding of these correlations; only an understanding of the mental sequences and the physical sequences separately and in their own terms.

(d) The natural laws that explain the movements of physical things, including human bodies, are those laws of physics that explain the behaviour of complex things by reference to the laws of motion governing their most simple elements. We can anticipate the logical outlines of acceptable physical theory, as it will gradually develop; but we are very far from knowing how the movements of very complex structures, studied by biologists, can be explained within the single physical theory, with its universal laws of motion. The human body is a supremely complex and sensitive physical structure, and Spinoza argues that we neither know nor can explain the powers which the human body possesses to act by itself, independently of intentions and conscious purposes. We do know *a priori* that all adequate explanation of reality, conceived as the domain of physical things, requires both universal laws of motion and a universal drive to self-maintenance in complex structures, which preserve their own nature while interacting with their environment. In the human body this drive to self-maintenance is appetite; and appetites in human beings are desires, when they are appetites of which we are, or can be, aware in thought.

We may intelligibly speak of a plant and of an animal as perceiving so-and-so and wanting so-and-so, in so far as in their interactions with their environment they are acted upon and react in accordance with their own nature. They receive information and they respond to the information received in accordance with their nature. We can therefore think of their behaviour and speak of them, in mental terms, as perceiving things and as having appetites. We can represent stimuli or inputs as perceptions, and the reactions traceable to their inner constitution and nature as appetites. In this sense we can think of all things, and not only human beings, as to a certain degree animated; this is the sense in which the plant registers the rays of the sun and seeks water. These facts about the plant can also be expressed in purely physical terms as physical interactions, and must be so expressed, if we are looking for adequate explanations of their observed physical changes and movements.

Spinoza's point in writing of all things as in a manner animated is to assimilate human perception and human desires to universal natural processes of interaction with the environment, and thereby to undermine the Cartesian theory of an abrupt discontinuity between the workings of the human soul and the behaviour of other things in the natural order. The observed behaviour and movements of human beings can be described in terms of inputs and outputs of energy of various kinds, and the movements thereby shown to be instances of laws of physics, chemistry and biology; with nothing said about the perceptions, desires, and intentions of the subject, or about the social and emotional significance of their behaviour. But we have to mention beliefs and desires, pleasure and pain, if we are to give adequate explanations of human behaviour as identified under descriptions that mark its social and emotional significance.

Appetite and perception, which become self-conscious as desires and beliefs in human beings, have a universal role in explaining the behaviour of objects in nature, and self-conscious desires and perceptions, which are one ordinary case of human desires and perceptions, may be regarded as a special case of interaction with the environment, from the perspective of a true philosophy.

(e) A thought is explained by being put into a sequence of thoughts which is by itself intelligible as connected thinking. Thinking is an activity, and we must not represent a sequence of thoughts as a sequence of discrete events, like a succession of images. Nor does the explanation of a thought consist in finding an experimentally-established correlation between independently identified events. Rather it consists in finding the missing steps in a process of thought which is otherwise fragmentary and incoherent as thought and therefore unintelligible.

Spinoza claims that bringing to consciousness the cause of a desire or belief, by an effort of reflection, is the discipline needed in order to correct the passive emotions, which we do not originate.

(f) There are two distinct orders of thinking, each of which are orders of intelligible thinking: the first is the order of the imagination, the second the order of the intellect. The first is governed by laws of the association of ideas, the second by the principles of logic. An adequate explanation of a man's particular desires, beliefs, and other propositional attitudes must refer them to one of these two orders, or to a combination of the two. In the order of the imagination a person's thoughts, and the emotions that are partly constituted by his thought, are determined by his perception of external things, and by his memories and associations. The capacity to trace and to criticize imaginative thinking is innate.

Persons have a radical conversion when they abandon their more general belief, consciously or unconsciously held, that they are peculiar islands in nature, not subject to natural laws, and when they apply to the classification of their own feelings the theory of the emotions which a consistent and systematic philosophy requires. Such a philosophy shows that the men and women whom we believe to be the causes of our suffering are not uncaused causes, nor do they have free will; rather they are links in an interminable chain of causes. We perceive other people differently, and their relations to us differently, when we no longer isolate them in our minds from the natural processes of thought, and the natural processes of bodily change and movement, which they exemplify.

More important still: we perceive our own perceptions of the world around us differently, and hence we perceive our own emotions and judgements differently, when we see our own emotions and behaviour as natural responses in the common order of nature. When this happens, we are substituting the order of the intellect, with its laws of coherent thought, for the order of the imagination, with its laws of the association of ideas. One is replacing the false sense of transcendence, implied by Descartes, with a sense of being in the world, of *être au monde* in the phenomenologist's sense. One is replacing the sense that the world of objects is presented to the independent thinking observer, to an intelligence detached from the body, who sees the world from no particular point of view within the world. A true self-consciousness makes one aware that one is looking at, and responding to, persons and things from a particular place among other persons and things, a place defined by bodily existence, and with a mind that functions, both in perceiving and in guiding action, under the limitations imposed by this embodiment.

If it is accepted that we have the two ways of thinking of reality, including ourselves – as a system of thinking things, and as a system of physical objects in space – the question about the equivalence of the two ways immediately arises, a famous crux in the interpretation of Spinoza. In one sense, or from one point of view, thought has a primacy: namely, from the point of view of the thinking subject, who reflects on his own thinking, and, following the order of the intellect, frees himself from attachment to his immediate environment. To have the power of reflective thought is to have the power of thinking about one's own thinking, in an indefinitely complex spiral of self-correction. From another point of view, that of the scientific observer looking for exact laws of nature, reality conceived as a system of physical things has a kind of primacy; because the world conceived as a physical system, in which human bodies are elements, is the first object of our exact inquiries and of our manipulations, under the important condition that our bodies are the instruments of our inquiries and of our manipulations.

The materialist will claim that every mental state of a person, and particularly every emotion, can also be represented as a physical condition; and when a state of a person is represented as a physical state, it is represented as a state that can in principle be exactly controlled by the application to the particular case of the laws of physics and chemistry. Reality conceived as a system of extended things is a domain in which exact and universal quantitative laws, experimentally testable, are to be found. The desire to control the mind–body state, and the knowledge of physical theory which exact control requires, plainly are themselves states of a person conceived as a thinking subject. A moralist and a philosopher try to change men's behaviour by producing thoughts about their thoughts, while a physician, using thought, typically tries to change men's behaviour by changing their bodily states.

20

The essential and often neglected insight which follows from Spinoza's metaphysical doctrine of the two attributes, is that there is no incompatibility, and no competition, between the two systems of explanation, the immaterialist and the materialist systems of explanation. They are both valid and indispensable, and each is independent of the other and complete in itself. Therefore there is no need, and no proper place, for the kind of arguments which have divided both psychiatrists and the lay public when materialist conceptions of personality are proposed. The fantasies and unconscious wishes and memories of a mentally disturbed person have their own causes in his past perceptions and imaginations and emotions, and the causal connections between them follow the laws of thought. To cause the patient to become aware of the operations of his own imagination in engendering his beliefs and his wishes will cause him at the same time to understand his own behaviour as the expression of these beliefs and wishes. If this is achieved, and he understands the desires and purposes manifested in his conduct, these desires and purposes will be modified by his understanding, at least to some extent. His fantasies and imaginations are constituted by the concepts familiar to him, and are expressed in his language, and are linked to his memories. His desires and beliefs, his fears and his other propositional attitudes, bear the marks of his culture and vocabulary, and of the habits of thought which he has formed, and of the unexamined, pre-conscious beliefs in which he was brought up. To explain one of his fantasies and imaginations, or of his more explicit and articulated desires and beliefs, is to situate it in a context of his thought and of his memories.

Sexuality provides the clearest untrivial illustration of Spinoza's theory. The sexual act may be described in terms of the various fantasies and desires that enter into the love-making; and these fantasies and desires will generally involve concepts, and an expressive vocabulary, which are culture-bound, and which are far from common to mankind. The sexual activity of an individual is imbued with his particular thought, his imagination, and his desire, and it reveals his individual mind with its weight of history. At the same time sexual activity is physical activity and its mechanisms are universally observable. We explain the sexual thoughts of the individual by supplying a wider context for them, which makes them intelligible as normal thought. The bodily processes we explain by the laws of physics and chemistry.

A man's passions may be so strong that he is unable to reflect and to substitute the order of the intellect for the order of the imagination in his thinking. His fear may be lessened by a chemical agent which acts on the physical state, which is the bodily aspect of his fear. There will be an adequate explanation within physiology of the chemical action on the nervous system and brain; but there is no intelligible and regular connection between the peculiar content of the thoughts that enter into his fears and the chemical transactions in his body. No very general correlation can be expected between an observed chemical transaction and the thoughts of men who have diverse languages, different conceptual schemes and memories, and different background knowledge; and such a correlation is in any case difficult to establish if a man's thoughts are not separately identifiable as discrete events, but only as steps in an activity of thought. When the full context is supplied, either the laws of association of ideas in the imagination or the laws of logic, or a combination of the two, will be discernible in the sequence of thought.

How a particular form of madness, or a particular form of neurosis, or any other aberrant state, is best treated in the present state of knowledge, is an empirical question, and cannot be profitably debated as an *a priori* issue. The *a priori* and philosophical claim, based on the double aspect theory, applies to the nature of adequate explanation; the theory prescribes what counts as a full theoretical understanding of thought, and what counts as a full theoretical understanding of physical and bodily states. There are evidently rough associations between some bodily changes, vaguely identified, and some changes in states of mind, vaguely identified. These are the rough associations which we learn by experience and on which we rely at a pre-theoretical level for practical purposes. But if experience suggests that my anger has caused my heart to race, the racing heart has to be explained as related to preceding bodily states by the laws of physics and chemistry, if a systematic, exact, and testable explanation is required. Singular causal judgements such as 'My anger has made my heart race' may be roughly true at their own level without being acceptable as possible parts of an adequate explanation. The judgement does not allude to a natural law, and the association noticed is not, and is not taken to be, an instance of one.

21

Spinoza's variant of materialism, stated from the standpoint of the active subject rather than of the observer, seems to me more than plausible, even though it is a speculation that runs far ahead of any firm knowledge in psychology which we possess. That explanation of thought assumes an entirely different form from explanation in physics: that thinking is an activity not analysable into discrete events, and that for this reason, among others, explanation of thought must always be entirely different from the explanation of physical processes: that our desires and beliefs are changed by reflection on their causes, and that to view our own emotions and desires with an enlightened theory of mental causation in mind is already to change these emotions and desires: that most of the thought that forms our ordinary beliefs and desires follows non-rational associations of ideas and is influenced by unrecognized emotions and memories: that self-knowledge, and the bringing to consciousness and to rational criticism of unconscious thought, and of the emotions that are formed by it, is the principal way to moral improvement: that human knowledge is limited by physical factors, more specifically, by the sense organs and the brain, and that we can in our rational moments make allowance for these limits: that human beings have not only the same physical structures as other creatures, but also have similar drives, as interpreted by biologists, and similar needs; that their recognition of their subordinate position in the vast natural order, and their emotional acceptance of this subordination, is a central virtue that leads to the other virtues, and particularly to tolerance: that the virtues necessary to sustaining a liberal society naturally come from a philosophy which stresses the narrow limits of human knowledge, and which stresses the fact that most human behaviour is governed by unconscious memories and by hatreds due to prejudice, and that it is not to be governed by rational calculation.

These doctrines are strengthened, and their direct relevance to morality reinforced, if the theory of evolution and of natural selection is added to the scientific background of Spinoza's naturalist ethics. With extraordinary insight Spinoza complicated the simple materialism of his contemporaries with his notion of self-maintenance of systems within systems and of the complex organization of different levels of living things. But his theory of knowledge, and therefore his moral theory, would have been more convincing if he had been able to represent the human brain and sense organs as having evolved gradually and as having conferred traceable advantages on the species, at least for a time, within the long evolutionary process. Secondly, the limits upon human knowledge, and powers of thought, no longer seem so certain and unalterable as they are within his theory, if accelerating additions to knowledge can be used to improve both the physical instrument of thought and thought itself.

22

Spinoza, like Aristotle, put public policy and political activity at the centre of morality. Unlike Aristotle, he explained both in his political works and in the *Ethics* the necessity of liberal institutions in an intelligent society. His principles prohibited bigotry and fanaticism, the denial of the right to dissent, and tyranny in any form; they prescribed the practical arts of political compromise, the defence of free thought, and the enjoyment of love and friendship and of active citizenship.

Spinoza believed that a mystical, or quasi-mystical, intellectual love of nature as the Creator can replace mystical emotions before a transcendent God. The phrase 'Deus Sive Natura' makes this point precisely. The dryness and thinness of a morality unsupported by the emotions that have as their object something transcendent seems to have a natural remedy: not exactly a nature mysticism, but certainly an exaltation and respect before the order and variety of nature.

These are vague ideas, associated with the word 'naturalism', and perhaps they are too vague for useful philosophical discussion. Certainly they need to be developed, and in a direction which is not anticipated in Spinoza's thought, which notoriously omits from its survey of the emotions, and of the activities of the mind, any account of aesthetic experience and works of creative imagination. Kant's *Critique of Judgement* is here the necessary text, because it very plausibly analyses the pleasure and exaltation which may be felt in the face of nature, both as an order that is understood and as an order that can never be wholly understood. Secondly, Kant associates this feeling for nature both with enjoyment of beauty and with the enjoyment of art; and he sketches a relation between the enjoyment of art, and between the emotions that are linked with works of the imagination on the one side, and with morality on the other. More specifically, he argues that aesthetic enjoyment of works of art includes an enjoyment of imaginative genius, and that the characteristic of genius is that its products seem to be not artificial and not man-made, and not the effects of contrivance; rather they seem to be the effects of some natural force. On the other side, in the enjoyment of natural beauty, we have the impression of some natural scenes being adapted and formed to please our imagination, as if we were in a prepared garden, designed for our pleasure, and expressing human feeling. Therefore aesthetic enjoyment closes the gap between the artificial, which can be made by genius to seem natural, and the natural, which sometimes is adapted to the pleasure of human perception and imagination, as it if were artificial.

This is a nature mysticism, typical of the eighteenth century, which Kant had peculiarly strong reasons for stressing; for he had represented morality as the overcoming of natural impulse and natural sentiment, and as being in its essence reason's defiance of natural inclination and natural enjoyment. There is therefore an immense strain, the strain of a necessarily divided nature, between rational morality and natural inclination. For Kant aesthetic experience is indispensable as a mediation between the demands of reason and the demands of pleasure and inclination, and also between the need for order and coherence on the one side and for wildness and the creative extravagances of imagination on the other. For this theory of early Romanticism, the landscape garden,or the cultivated ruin in the park, or the folly, are the images of an ideal relation between man and the rest of nature, from which he is otherwise alienated.

This Romantic idea of the need to recapture naturalness, otherwise lost in the exercise of reason, comes near to explaining the metaphysical emotions which can take the place of those associated with transcendental religions; particularly Kant's theory of genius and of originality in the imagination as being the channel through which natural insights, otherwise lost, return to the human mind, as it were, unobserved and by unknown paths. We seem to ourselves to be brought into contact with a permanent natural order through works of imaginative art, whether literature, music, or painting; there occurs the familiar feeling that works of a genius reveal an otherwise concealed or muffled reality, not accessible to science or to any conscious reflection.

The claims of morality seem not easily reconciled with the idea of an individual's life, and the life of the species as a whole, as small episodes in a vast natural process, unless the episode is given a special place within the natural process: and understanding here includes reason and the imagination also. Aristotle argued that in the exercise of theoretical reason in the pursuit of truth, human beings play the immortal as far as is possible for them, and are absorbed in permanent realities. He represents this activity as the summit of achievement, the highest virtue. Spinoza's suggested escape from transience is through natural knowledge and a mystical sense of the unity of nature, which will enable some people to have a vision of a permanent order and to identify themselves with it, at least through their inquiries. This certainly is one relief from transience, and an old and very well-known one. But I think that for many persons those emotional experiences which can be called aesthetic are also escapes from a sense of triviality and impermanence, and in this respect have some of the force attributed to mystical experiences. They suggest to the mind, while the experience lasts, not only an exaltation, but also the thought of being in contact with some permanent reality or pattern. This is a vague thought, but it is a familiar one both in experience and in literature.

A final observation: these two intellectually persuasive theories of morality, Aristotle's and Spinoza's, rest upon different visions of human life. Although Aristotle represents theoretical interest in eternal realities as the highest virtue, he still thinks of a single human life, taken as a whole, as constituting a good or a bad total performance, including the exercise of theoretical reason within the performance. He imparts a strong sense, to be expected in a biologist, of the limited and natural span of a life and of the completion of successful activity which may be achieved within that temporal span. One might say, in caricature, that the argument of the Nicomachean Ethics leads the reader to view a human life, and particularly his own, from the standpoint of his eventual obituarist.

Spinoza does not lead one to assess an individual's life as an outstanding performance, or as a poor performance, within its natural constraints, because he has a different idea of time and of our experience of it. It is not the total performance within an individual's life that counts, but the occasions of transcendence, when a person is able to understand things, including himself, *sub specie aeternitatis*, rather than *sub specie durationis*. Behind the ordinarily experienced temporal order and the temporal units, such as a human lifetime, there is an intellectual order with units that are the significant units within systematic theory; and a desire for understanding and enjoyment of this intellectual order should override all other interests.

3

Two Kinds of Explanation

or Seeing Double

1

History as an inquiry is not to be assimilated to the natural sciences, and historians should not seriously claim to be scientific. The events and trends that compose human history do not illustrate ascertainable general laws governing all human history, as the events in physical systems illustrate general laws governing all plysical systems. Thirdly, the actions and sentiments of individuals in history, and also of social groups, have to be understood in a way that is distinctive and characteristic of historical understanding; it is different particularly in bringing out, as vividly as possible, the peculiar and transient idiosyncrasy of the individual or social group under study. This is the precision aimed at, and not the precision of scientific generality. I shall describe and advocate a philosophical position from which the truth of these three propositions could be inferred. Their relevance to morality is explained in chapters 6 and 7.

2

If I press my eyeballs while standing in front of a lighted candle, I shall usually see two lighted candles where previously I had seen one. I would know that I had interfered with the bodily mechanism which enables me to identify the objects before me and that enables me to handle them successfully. If I had been instructed in the physiology of perception, I would also know why the pressing of my eyeballs had precisely this effect of making me see double; I would be able to describe in some detail the mechanisms at work, and I would be able to specify the causes of the distortion. I would not for a moment believe that there were two candles before me, because I have had sufficient experience of the working of my eye to make allowances for the physical effect. If I were to explain my beliefs about the identity of the objects before me, I would reply with further relevant beliefs and items of knowledge about my observing self and about the appearance of relevant things around me, which, taken together, explain my present judgement; and this kind of explanation could be called giving the grounds of my belief, at least when the explanation is offered under these conditions. The mechanisms of my body, including the brain and central nervous system, are used by me both in exploring objects external to me and in making changes in them, and also in investigating and changing the accessible mechanisms of my body. I use the complex instrument with functions according to the universal laws of physics and of chemistry, forming my perceptual beliefs in association with the instrument's interactions with the physical environment.

This is how we are placed in the world as observers of it. In order to explore and to observe the world we have to move, and to move parts of the body, eyes, hands, legs, and also to touch and move objects. We so act with specific intentions, resolved to notice precisely what happens as the effect of our actions. About such intentional actions yet another question – 'Why?' – can be asked, and this calls for an answer by reference to the beliefs and desires which, taken together, move us to take the action that we did.

The reasons that moved me to action, like the reasons that made me believe that there was only one candle, may be far from explicitly rehearsed. I may know that I have good reasons for the belief and also good reasons for the action, while I may have great difficulty in disentangling and making explicit what the reasons are. There may be a number of considerations of unequal weight and influence, stored and compressed in my mind, which need to be quoted in giving any sufficient explanation of my belief and of my action. But there are occasions of difficulty and uncertainty when I must explicitly review the considerations for and against a suggested belief and a suggested action, and also situations where, confronting a variety of conflicting evidence or a variety of conflicting reasons for action, I must formulate some definite conclusion. These are occasions on which I must brood on considerations for and against, and on which salient reasons become fully explicit and present to the subject's mind, or as fully explicit as reasons ever become.

3

There are two standpoints from which the relation between reasons and conclusion in the brooding situation can be examined, whether the conclusion is a practical intention or a belief; from the standpoint of the subject who is making clear to himself what his reasons are at the time of drawing his conclusions, and from the standpoint of the subject looking back on a past conclusion and explaining to himself why he decided as he did. To these two standpoints another must be added: the standpoint of an observer, who is not the thinking subject, and who is not in a position to know directly, or to recall directly, what the reasons were which were explicitly present to the subject's mind and which led him, or seem to have led him, to his conclusion. Both for knowledge of the reasons that led to a conclusion in a contemporary case of brooding, and for retrospective explanation, the observer must rely on the subject's testimony and on other external evidence. The question 'Why?' is asked in the first person singular of the present tense about a belief and an intention, or course of action, when a man needs to clear his mind about what he believes on a particular topic and about what he will do in a particular situation. This posing of the question in the first person of the present tense is certainly not marginal and exceptional. If action alone is considered, the first person of the present form of the question 'Why?' might even be called central rather than the retrospective question, or the question 'Why?' asked by an observer.

In the Nicomachean Ethics Aristotle represents the process of brooding on the proper target of one's conduct as the first and fundamental form of practical reasoning. Persons are frequently confused in their own minds both about what they want and about what they intend to achieve, and they give incorrect descriptions to themselves of the ends that they are pursuing. For example, they tell themselves that before all things they want to be rich, when in fact they want before all things some of the anticipated consequences of being rich. Observation of their behaviour or further questioning may show that money is for them only a means to an end; but they do not realise this, and in consequence they are apt to act in ways which defeat their own ends. In consequence their life, taken as a whole, is one of unhappiness and of unfulfilled potentialities.

It is a natural error, often supported by false philosophies of mind, that people must know what they want, and if they have formed intentions, they must always know, beyond the possibility of error, what their own intentions are. Even without the complexities of self-deception, sheer misconception of the objects of propositional attitudes, including desire, is a familiar kind of failure in self-knowledge. The errors to which we are liable here are typically not trivial, a mere mismatching of names, but substantial. We mistake the objects of our fears, and misunderstand the reaons for our own passions. We find it difficult to pick out the elements or features in a situation which explain our sadness and gloom, and skill and discipline are needed if we are to be clear about what we are enjoying, or what gives us deep satisfaction, in some scene in which we are involved, or in something that we are reading or hearing. 'What do I want to achieve?', 'What do I fear here?', 'What do I dislike about this?', 'What do I really enjoy, as opposed to those things which I persuade myself that I like?', 'What do I respect?', 'What do I admire?', 'What do I really intend to do about this, as opposed to merely wishing or hoping?' – these are all questions about which a person may think carefully. In answering them in any difficult case, he has to rehearse causal, or quasi-causal, hypotheses about what would be the case if one or the other feature of the object or situation before him were changed. He has to review possibilities and alternatives, and he cannot avoid counterfactual speculations if he is to find accurate, and sufficiently complete, answers to these questions, and the questions are directly relevant to conduct.

4

Some years ago, in 'Subjunctive Conditionals', published in *Analysis*, 9 (1949), 9–14; republished in 'Freedom of Mind' (Oxford University Press, 1972), confronting the problem of singular counterfactuals as an epistemological problem, I suggested that they had an ineliminable place in practical deliberation, which is a process of reviewing possible future worlds. Therefore some account of the normal conditions of their verification or falsification has to be given, even if the normal conditions of their verification preclude them from being acceptable in scientific theory. Partly because they are not regularly testable by experiment and observation, they were not a part of the unified language of science as reconstructed by W. V. Quine and other philosophical logicians. Their truth conditions are not uniformly and clearly specified, and vary with the context in which they are employed. But they have an indispensable part not only in practical calculations and causal judgements prior to action and non-causal judgements that impute responsibility in a rational way, but also in the formation of sentiments and attitudes and in reflections on them. In making clear and explicit the reasons for his hopes, fears, wishes, admirations, regrets, sadness, happiness and so forth, a person reflects on the conditions under which his sentiments and attitudes would change. He is then thinking counterfactually.

In the brooding situation, in which a person considers the reasons for his contemporary desires, beliefs, intentions and attitudes, the reasons that explain his state of mind are both grounds and causes. When he recalls later what made him have the desires, beliefs, intentions and sentiments which were explicitly his at the time, and the weight that he gave to reason in his explicit thinking, he can separate the normative question of whether they were good grounds from the historical question of whether he has accurately specified the considerations that were at work in his thinking, and whether his explicit reasoning masked other considerations present to his mind, and whether he was self-deceived. He is asking himself whether, if the situation had been different in such-and-such respects, his desires, beliefs, intentions and sentiments would have been different in such-and-such other respects; he is looking for a connection, or connections, between features of his previous thought and the features of the desire, belief or intention which is to be explained. That the notions of ground and cause should be confounded, or brought together, has often been a criticism of the rationalist philosophy brought forward by empiricists. But the elementary notion of cause, employed in calculations and ordinary manipulations and in most practical reasoning, unavoidably brings together ground and cause, as one shifts from the standpoint of initiating subject and agent to that of objective explanation of observed change.

5

When the dogmas of empiricist philosophy are put on one side, it is not difficult to see what kind of connection between reason and conclusion is in question, and how the counterfactual propositions are supported. We are constantly familiar with conditional intentions, and also with conditional beliefs and desires. We resolve to do something provided that such-and-such conditions are satisfied, and we will believe something if such-and-such evidence comes in, and we want something if it has such-and-such a feature and not otherwise. The singular counterfactual propositions are explicitly supported by conditional intentions in cases where the intention (or desire or belief) has been formed as the outcome of explicit reasoning, that is, in the brooding situation; for then the subject knows, or is in a position to know, that he formed the intention because of such-and-such considerations. The question 'What supports the singular counterfactual proposition?' is answered by 'The original intention itself, which at its formation was in this respect conditional.' One naturally thinks of counterfactual judgements as requiring support, in the sense that there should be an indirect means of satisfying oneself of their truth or falsity, since a direct means of testing them is normally excluded. When a person is speculating about the connection between his own intentions and attitudes, and when he is citing these connections as explanations, he is often in the exceptional position of knowing directly what conditions surrounded his original intentions and attitudes, while other persons, observing him, can only know from his testimony and by inference from parallel cases. Unless he has forgotten, the subject usually knows about the surrounding context of calculation in which his intention was on a particular occasion formed, and he can therefore explain why his intention assumed the particular form that it did, and under what conditions it would have been in certain respects different. He would be in a specially good position to know this if his intention or attitude had emerged from a situation of brooding.

Evidently a person explaining his own actions, intentions and attitudes is still explaining the actions and attitudes of an observed natural object, whose intentions and attitudes conform to natural tendencies; and he knows this. He is not infallible in his counterfactual judgements and in his explanations of himself, and he knows that he is liable on occasion to be self-deceived. It is sometimes difficult for him to be sure that what he thinks was his reason was in fact his reason, and difficult to be sure that he would have reacted with such-and-such a change of attitude under certain other conditions. The contrasting and controlling source of knowledge is observation, and particularly observation of uniform, or nearly uniform, connections between activating reasons and resulting intentions, attitudes and sentiments. These uniformities constitute supporting grounds for counterfactual judgements alongside the counterfactual judgements which emerge directly from processes of deliberation; and evidently the two sources of knowledge will sometimes be in conflict, pointing to contrary counterfactual judgements. Sometimes it will seem that a person's belief, desire or intention is to be explained by considerations present to his mind which are altogether exceptional and which are peculiar to this occasion. The counterfactual judgement is supported by a clear conditional intention, which on this occasion is taken to outweigh the observed uniformities of past behaviour in parallel cases. At other times it will seem undeniable, in view of the record, that the reasons that a man is offering to himself and to others to explain his intentions are mere rationalizations; he would not have changed his attitude if the circumstances had been different in the one respect which he picks out as the determining one.

6

The alteration and balance between the two kinds of support for counterfactual judgements is an aspect of the conjugation of the psychological verbs which pick out propositional attitudes such as 'I want', 'I believe', 'I fear', 'I hope', and which move from first person to second or third. It is open to everyone to think of himself or to observe himself, from the standpoint of a detached observer of his actual behaviour and from the records of the past: just as anyone may pause to reflect on his desires, beliefs and intentions, and on his fears and hopes, as he does in the brooding situation. When a person forms his plans for the future and firmly fixes his intentions, he needs to assure himself that, in all likelihood, he will actually do what he now says to himself that he will do; he needs to be sure that his intention really is an intention and not just a vague aspiration or wish. If the publicly accessible record showed that he had repeatedly formed similar intentions which never issued in action, because he subsequently changed his mind, or because he lost his nerve, there would be reason to doubt that his present intention was more than a mere wish; and this is a reason which should cause the subject to doubt also, because he can be an observer of himself, as others can. He who tells others that he will come to the meeting tomorrow, and that they can be sure of this because he is sure, still has no magical certainty about the future; his subjective assurance is checkable against the probabilities established by induction from past performances.

The whole vocabulary of propositional attitudes – of desire, belief, fear, hope, anger, regret and so forth – has this same characteristic, and for the same reasons: there is always an interplay between the direct assurance of the subject and the external criteria applied by observers, including the subject himself. This is the epistemological reflection of the 'being in the world' of persons, who are both language-using, and therefore reflective, agents, and also observers of the other medium-sized objects, including other persons, whom they try to understand and to control for practical purposes. When a person speaks, he knows in advance what he will say, and this knowledge is not acquired by observation, but comes to him from his intention. The words that he actually utters and that he hears may diverge from his intention, and the explanation may be a slip of the tongue, a quasi-mechanical fault in the execution of his intention. He might discover that he is unable to pronounce a word as he should and as he intended; his body does not follow his intention. Alternatively he may change his mind at the last moment of utterance and the word that then issues from his lips is different from the originally intended word. The borderline that divides the two divergences from the original intention may sometimes be very hard to discern, if we are trying to give an ordinary, pre-theoretical, causal explanation of the previously unintended word being uttered. The subject himself may not know on some occasions whether it was a case of a mere physical malfunctioning or a change of mind at the last moment. He may be uncertain precisely because most intentions are not fully explicit and articulated, and the change of mind might have occurred without being brought into full consciousness. There is no guarantee that on all occasions a clear and reasonably certain account of what occurred can be obtained.

The vocabulary that distinguishes the various propositional attitudes, including beliefs, desires and intentions, requires that the reasons taken by the subject to explain a specific attitude should be of a kind that is compatible with that specific attitude. If there is not the required connection between the explaining cause and reason and the resulting attitude, as the subject conceives them, he will begin to doubt his identification of the attitude. There is nothing mysterious about this lack of the prescribed Humean disconnection between the explaining cause and the explained effect, if one recalls the use of the psychological vocabulary in the first person singular of the present tense alongside its other use. The cause that explains the propositional attitude, if the cause is a belief or desire or another propositional attitude, must be of a kind that fits into a sequence of thought which the subject might follow. It may be true that I believe something, or that I want something, because I have been hypnotized with this effect. Then there is not the required connection between the cause and the effect; but in these circumstances it still will not be true that I, the subject, believe that this is the best explanation of my belief or desire. There will be another explanation, which I wrongly believe to be the correct explanation in terms of other beliefs and desires which are mine. This will be a rationalization of my belief or desire, which I shall think of as fitting into the system of my beliefs and desires. The connection between the hypnotism and the desire or belief is not an intelligible connection, in the implied sense, precisely because it satisfies the requirement of Humean disconnection, and because it is not a conceivable part of a process of deliberation. The causal connection can be described as 'mechanical'. The hypothetical propositions cannot occur in the first person as statements of conditional intentions; they would be unintelligible in this guise, because they do not form part of a conceivable thought-process ending with this conditional attitude.

We may think that we know why we have the beliefs and desires that we do, but we are sometimes wrong or partly wrong. But there is good reason to believe, first, that persons in general are in the majority of cases not in error when they state the causes of their intentions, desires and attitudes, and, secondly, that any particular person is in general not in error when he states the causes of his intentions, desires and beliefs; and that this holds true for other propositional attitudes also. To recur to the original example: there is the situation in which I wrongly believe that I am seeing two candles, when this belief is the effect of a physical cause of which I am ignorant. But if and when I become aware of this causal connection, the propositional attitude is to some degree and in some way modified because of this awareness. The belief is checked by reflection on the unrespectable character of its apparent cause.

We all do explicitly review our beliefs and desires, and deliberate about them, and at the same time we are liable to be partly ignorant of causes external to our thought which are determining our desires and beliefs. There is always a potential conflict between the reasons present to our mind as causing a belief or desire and the apparent causes external to our conscious, or unconscious, thinking; therefore there is always a potential conflict between the hypothetical propositions supported by the subject's intentions and the hypothetical propositions supported by general propositions. It is a recurrent philosophical error to take either side as permanently dominant, the subjective or the objective. The error may take the form of interpreting statements of intention as incorrigible, or alternatively of supposing that all specifications of reasons for attitudes or actions might be interpreted as rationalizations, because the real causes are to be found elsewhere and in conditions external to the subject's thought. Both theories cut across the entrenched uses of the psychological vocabulary. The shift from the first person to the second and third persons is the syntactical expression of changes of standpoint from which a state of mind can be attributed, and, taken together with changes of tense, the conjugation indicates the kind of support that the attribution may be expected to claim, if challenged. The alternation between the standpoints is not only a check on claims to incorrigibility for one kind of knowledge or the other; it is also a reflection of the fact, so easily obscured, that we each exist as natural objects, observably conforming to natural laws, and also as natural objects which have the peculiar gift of reflecting on our states of mind, and of applying the knowledge of causes that we acquire to modify our states of mind.

7

This feedback of knowledge through the loop of reflective thinking introduces a complexity into the description of mental states which has no parallel in the description of physical states, that is, of states known only by observation and experiment. Our recognition of this added complexity, and of its peculiarity, is sometimes called an awareness of freedom, in a sense in which only thinking beings are free. The consequence of the added complexity of reflection is that the very same observable state of two persons, when classified from the observer's standpoint, will constitute different states of mind from the standpoint of the subjects; for their knowledge or belief about the nature and causes of the observable state will in part determine what their states of mind are. This is just another aspect of the familiar fact that actions by two persons may be identical when seen from the observer's standpoint, but different when the agents' understanding of their situations, and their intentions, are different. The distinction between the same publicly observable action, performed on two occasions or by two persons, and the different thought or intentions animating it, is one instance of a more general relation between the subject's reflections on his observable state and his observable state. The contrast between the thought about the action or sentiment, and the observable action or manifestation of the sentiment, constitutes, and creates, that sense of freedom which men take to be peculiar to themselves.

8

This contrast has been stated in different ways by philosophers, and one aspect of the contrast is precisely that distinction between human culture and language, vastly various in history and in geography, and a common biological inheritance. This is the distinction which provides one ground for viewing historical method as autonomous and as entirely different from the methods of natural science. The claim has been that historians aim to recapture and reproduce the thought of particular people and periods in the past with all their idiosyncrasies and distinguishing marks, and that they both are, and should be, interested in particularities and nuances of styles and manners and local customs, and not at all in abstract generalizations about human affairs. Humanistic studies are essentially concerned with the varieties of languages in which men have cast their thought, each of them with its distinctive idioms and imagery, formed by the pressure of the particular memories and transmitted customs of one social order.

My argument is intended to show that the distinction between the methods and aims of history, as a humanistic study, and the methods and aims of the natural sciences rests on a more fundamental distinction: namely, that between reflexive, or intentional knowledge, which is not knowledge by observation, and knowledge by observation. This distinction in turn has its foundation in the natural powers of people as capable, because of the power of speech, of reflecting on their actions and feelings, and of planning their future actions and attitudes. But in the evolution of intelligence in the species the power of speech has for some reason been developed as a divisive power, which splits the species into comparatively uncommunicating groups. It seems to be essential to the power of speech that natural languages should hold groups together by exclusion, and that they should thereby contribute to a 'false speciation', in Erik Erikson's words. Whatever the advantage to the species of this splitting into many exclusive groups by language and culture, the effect has been to intensify the contrast between the observed and scientifically testable dispositions and states of the organism and the dispositions and states of the organism whose nature is in part dependent on the subject's recognition of them. Both the particular vocabulary used in the discrimination of emotions and attitudes, and the vocabulary used to discriminate customary forms of behaviour, may substantially modify the subject's conception of his emotions and of his actions. Modifying his conceptions, and modifying the way that he represents to himself and to others his actions and reactions, the idiosyncrasies of his language must enter into his direct experience; and a full allowance has to be made for these idiosyncrasies if an adequate description is to be given of his feelings and motives and conduct.

Adequacy of description has to be relative to some interest in view. The interest that demands an intentional description, taking account of the subject's representation of himself to himself, is not a contingent and dispensable interest, as if it just happened that we are interested in history as well as in natural science. The interest arises from the very existence of practical reasoning, from the mere fact that we make considered decisions, and also reflect on the decisions that we have made, and on the reasons for them. This is a fact, so elementary as to be scarcely noticeable, which has no regular place in most standard accounts of causal reasoning. That explanations of desires and beliefs, and of the decisions that issue from them and that are explained by them, fit into a rational framework is often acknowledged; but acknowledged often with the wrong implication: that the rational explanation is not any kind of causal explanation, because causal explanations require the support of a presumed natural law. The older uses of the word 'cause', present in Descartes, Spinoza and Leibniz, allow that explanations in the context of practical reasoning are still causal explanations, because the counterfactual implications are still open to challenge from the evidence of parallel instances. A historian who constructs a narrative that shows the consequences of his protagonists' actions is employing a notion of cause which leaves him open to challenge from parallel instances in history. But he is not aiming at a precision in his counterfactual speculations, or a testability, which would satisfy a scientist, who is usually interested in building a theory that will yield precise measurements.

Experiment is the prerequisite of the discovery of natural laws, and of the precision which the discovery of natural laws makes possible. The power of reflexive thinking, the power that gives us our sense of freedom, has the effect that the experimental inputs will have modified consequences when the experimental subject knows that he is the victim of the experiment. Reflexive thought sets a limit to the possibilities of manipulating desires and beliefs, as normal intentional states, whether the manipulation is for the sake of scientific theory or for other ends. Our sense of freedom is an awareness that we have this power to perceive, and to discount, manipulation, and that in this sense we are not helpless in the face of external causes, in respect at least of our beliefs and desires and similar propositional attitudes. Coming to understand what makes me want something which at the same time I think bad and which I therefore wish that I did not want, I shall often be in a better position to satisfy my second-order desire in virtue of my knowledge of the cause of the first-order desire.

When we wish to have a strictly deterministic account of human behaviour, and of bodily movements and changes, we can abstract from all intentional descriptions of human behaviour and look for experimentally testable correlations that are reasonably precise and that mention only observable characteristics. The experiments will be repeatable, and some of the correlations discovered will be accepted as equally reliable among Amazonian tribes as they are in Stockholm or Cambridge, Mass. The correlations of physiology, and of those parts of cognitive and clinical psychology that use only the concepts of physiology, are of this character. But the social sciences are not of this character, in so far as they mention beliefs and sentiments and specify the content of beliefs independently of their observable manifestations.

Therefore either the social sciences have to be abstract and scientific or a social scientist must be content with the unscientific character of historical analysis and of interpretative anthropology and of other humanistic studies, such as linguistics and jurisprudence. They must be content with the Vichian studies, which Vico called, comprehensively, philology, if they are to study the diverse social structures and systems of belief which men have formed and are still forming. In spite of the dreams of empiricist philosophers from Hume and Mill onwards, there will not be a social science which is an extension of the true natural sciences into the domain of belief and custom. This prophecy of mine does not rest on a metaphysical claim that there is some division in reality, on an ontological dualism. It rests on an observation about human knowledge, and the forms which it naturally takes, because we happen to have the peculiar and limited powers of perception and of thoughtful behaviour that we do have. The framework of determinism embraces the objects of observations, and intentional knowledge, the outcome of reflection, has a different framework. The power of reflection, and the power to learn a language which is part of it, are natural endowments embodied in some still largely unknown structures of the brain, as the power of visual discrimination is embodied in the eye. It is this power to which men are referring, whether they know it or not, when they speak of the kind of freedom which only human beings, among the known species of animal, enjoy, and which they can still develop and exploit.

4

Morality and Pessimism

British utilitarianism was a school of moral thought, and a school also of general philosophy, which set out to do good in the world, even though it was only a philosophy; and it may even be judged to have succeeded in large part over many years in this aim. It is certainly not easy, and perhaps it is not possible, to calculate the real effect upon our lives of any new system of moral ideas and of any new philosophy. But the utilitarian philosophy brought new interests into the study of political economy: into the theory and practice of public administration: into the rhetoric, and into the programmes, of movements of political and social reform in Britain. Indeed the utilitarian philosophy became part of the ordinary furniture of the minds of those enlightened persons, who would criticize institutions, not from the standpoint of one of the Christian churches, but from a secular point of view. As represented by Sidgwick at Cambridge, and in the minds of liberal and radical social reformers everywhere, the utilitarian philosophy was until quite recently a constant support for progressive social policies. Even the rare and strange adaptation of utilitarianism, which appeared in the last chapter of G. E. Moore's *Principia Ethica*, pointed towards liberal and improving policies: at least it did in the minds of Keynes and of Leonard Woolf and of others whose lives were seriously influenced by Moore. Moore himself wrote of his own moral conclusions as prescribing the aims of social policy, and, like Mill, he was marking the target of social improvements. The utilitarian philosophy, before the first world war and for many years after it – perhaps even until 1939 – was still a bold, innovative, even a subversive doctrine, with a record of successful social criticism behind it. I believe that it is losing this role.

Utilitarianism has always been a comparatively clear moral theory, with a simple core and central notion, easily grasped and easily translated into practical terms. Its essential instruction goes like this: when assessing the value of institutions, habits, conventions, manners, rules and laws, and also when considering the merits of individual actions or policies, turn your attention to the actual or probable states of mind of the persons who are, or will be, affected by them: that is all you need to consider in your assessments. In a final analysis, nothing else counts but the states of mind, and perhaps, more narrowly, the states of feeling, of persons; or, more generously in Bentham and G. E. Moore, of sentient creatures. Anything else that one might consider, in the indefinite range of natural and man-made things, is to be reckoned as mere machinery, as only a possible instrument for producing the all-important – literally all-important – states of feeling. From this moral standpoint, the whole machinery of the natural order, other than states of mind, just is machinery, useful or harmful in proportion as it promotes or prevents desired states of feeling.

For a utilitarian, the moral standpoint, which is to govern all our actions, places human beings at the very centre of the universe, with their states of feeling as the source of all value in the world. If the species perished, to the last man, or if the last persons became impassible and devoid of feeling, things would become cold and indifferent and neutral, from the moral point of view; whether this or that other unfeeling species survived or perished, plants, stars and galaxies would then be of no consequence. Destruction of things is evil only in so far as it is, or will be, felt as a loss by sentient beings.

This doctrine may reasonably be criticized in two contrary ways: first, as involving a kind of arrogance in the face of nature, an arrogance that is intelligible only if the doctrine is seen as a residue of the Christian account of our species' peculiar relation to the Creator. Without the Christian story it seems to entail a strangely arbitrary narrowing of moral interest. Is the destruction, for instance, of a species in nature to be avoided, as a great evil, only or principally because of the loss of the pleasure that sentient beings may derive from the species? May the natural order be framed by human beings for their comfort and pleasure without any restriction other than the comfort and pleasure of future human beings? Perhaps there is no rational procedure for answering these questions. But it is strange to answer them with a confident 'Yes'. On the other hand the doctrine that only our feelings are morally significant may be thought, on the contrary, to belittle us: for it makes morality, the system of rights, duties and obligations, a kind of psychical engineering, which shows the way to induce desired or valued states of mind. This suggests, as a corollary, that people might be trained, moulded, even bred, with a view to their experiencing the kinds of feeling that alone lend value to their morally neutral surroundings. With advancing knowledge states of the soul might be controlled by chemical means, and the valuable experiences of the inner life may be best prolonged and protected by a medical technique. So the original sense of the sovereign importance of human beings, and of their feelings, has been converted by exaggeration into its opposite: a sense that these original ends of action are, or may soon become, comparatively manageable problems in applied science.

From the standpoint of philosophy, in a full, old-fashioned sense of that word, we have moved slowly, stage by stage, in the years since 1914, into a different world of thought from that which most of Leslie Stephen's contemporaries inhabited; and by a 'world of thought' here I mean the set of conditioning assumptions which any European, who thought in a philosophical way about morality, would have in mind before he started to think, assumptions that he probably would not examine one by one, and that he would with difficulty make explicit to himself. One such asumption was that, even if the transcendental claims of Christianity have been denied, any serious thought about morality must acknowledge the absolute exceptionalness of human beings, the unique dignity and worth of this species among otherwise speechless, inattentive things, and their uniquely open future; how otherwise can morality have its overriding claims? A second assumption, explicit in J. S. Mill, and unchallenged by his utilitarian successors, was that both emotional sensitiveness, and intelligence in the calculation of consequences, can be expected to multiply and increase, as moral enlightenment spreads and as standards of education improve, into an indefinite and open future. In this open future there will be less avoidable waste of human happiness, less unconsidered destruction of positive and valued feelings, as the human sciences develop and superstitions become weaker and softer. The story of the past – this is the assumption – is essentially the story of moral waste, of a lack of clear planning and contrivance, of always repeated losses of happiness because no one methodically added the emotional gains and losses, with a clear head and undistracted by moral prejudices. The modern utilitarian policy-makers will be careful social economists, and their planning mistakes will be progressively corrigible ones; so there is no reason why there should not be a steadily rising balance of positive over negative feelings in all societies that have a rational computational morality. A new era of development is possible, the equivalent in morality of high technology in production.

This implicit optimism has been lost, not so much because of philosophical arguments but perhaps rather because of the hideous face of political events. Persecutions, massacres and wars have been coolly justified by calculations of the long-range benefit to mankind; and political pragmatists, in the advanced countries, using cost–benefit analyses prepared for them by gifted professors, continue to burn and destroy. The utilitarian habit of mind has brought with it a new abstract cruelty in politics, a dull, destructive political righteousness: mechanical, quantitative thinking, leaden loveless minds setting out their moral calculations in leaden abstract prose, and more civilized and more superstitious people destroyed because of enlightened calculations that have proved wrong. Suppose a typical situation of political decision, typical, that is, of the present, and likely to be typical of the immediate future; an expert adviser has to present a set of possible policies between which a final choice has to be made; advantages and disadvantages of various outcomes are to be calculated, and a balance is to be struck. The methods of calculation may be quite sophisticated, and very disparate items may appear in the columns of gain and loss. The death of groups of persons may, for example, be balanced as a loss against a very considerable gain in amenity to be handed down to posterity; or a loss of liberty among one group may be balanced against a very great relief from poverty for another. Such calculations are the everyday stuff of political decision, and they seem to require a common measure that enables qualitatively unrelated effects to be held in balance. The need to calculate in this manner, and to do so convincingly, plainly becomes greater as the area of government decision is widened, and as the applied social sciences render remote effects more computable.

Given that the vast new powers of government are in any case going to be used, and given that remote and collateral effects of policies are no longer utterly incalculable, and therefore to be neglected, a common measure to strike a balance is certain to be asked for and to be used; and apparently incommensurable interests wil be brought together under this common measure. The utilitarian doctrine, insisting that there is a common measure of those gains and losses, which superficially seem incommensurable, is in any case called into being by the new conditions of political calculation. Any of the original defects in the doctrine will now be blown up, as a photograph is blown up, and made clearly visible in action.

For Machiavelli and his contemporaries, a political calculation was still a fairly simple computation of intended consequences, not unlike the stratagems of private intrigue. He and his contemporaries had no thought that a political calculation might issue in a plan for the future of a whole society or nation, with all kinds of dissimilar side-effects allowed for, and fed into the computation. Computation by a common measure now seems the most orthodox way to think in politics, although this kind of computation had originally been almost scandalous. At first the scandal and surprise lingered around the notion that moral requirements, and moral outrages, could be represented as commensurable gains and losses along a single scale. Yet now those who talk about being responsible in political decision believe that the moral issues must be represented on a common scale, if they are to be counted at all. How can the future of an advanced society be reasonably discussed and planned, if not on this assumption? To others, and particularly to many of the young in America and in Europe, who would not quote Burke, it seems now obvious that the large-scale computations in modern politics and social planning bring with them a coarseness and grossness of moral feeling, a blunting of sensibility, and a suppression of individual discrimination and gentleness, which are a price that they will not pay for the benefits of clear calculation. Their point is worth considering: perhaps it can be given a philosophical basis.

To go back to the beginnings of moral theory: as a non-committal starting-point, it may be agreed that we all assess ourselves, and other people, as having behaved well or badly, on a particular occasion, or for a tract of time, or taking a lifetime as a whole. We similarly assess courses of action, and even whole ways of life, that are open to us before we make a decision. The more fundamental and overriding assessments, in relation to which all other assessments of persons are subsidiary and conditional, we call moral assessments, just because we count them as unconditional and overriding. The goodness or badness imputed may be imputed as a characteristic of persons, or of their actions, their decisions and their policies, or of their character and their dispositions, or of their lives and ways of life. Let me take the assessment of persons as the starting-point. When we assess ourselves or others in some limited role or capacity, as performing well or ill in that role or capacity, the assessment is not fundamental and unconditional; the assessment gives guidance only to someone who wants to have that role or to act in that capacity, or who wants to make use of someone who does. But if we assess persons as good or bad without further qualification or limitation, merely as human beings, and similarly also their decisions, policies, characters, dispositions, ways of life, as being good or bad without qualification, then our assessments have unconditional implications in respect of what should and should not be done, and of what people should, and should not be like, of their character, dispositions and way of life. A human being has the power to reflect on what kind of person he wants to be, and to try to act accordingly, within the limits of his circumstances. His more considered practical choices, and the conflicts that accompany them, will show what he holds to be intrinsically worth pursuing, and will therefore reveal his fundamental moral beliefs.

I believe that all I have so far said about this starting-point of moral philosophy is non-committal between different theories, and is innocent and unquestion-begging, and will be, or ought to be, accepted by moral philosophers of quite different persuasions, including the utilitarians. I believe this, because the various classical moral philosophies can all be formulated within this non-committal framework. Each moral philosophy singles out some ultimate ground or grounds for unconditional praise of persons, and prescribes the ultimate grounds for preferring one way of life to another. This is no less true of a utilitarian ethics than of any other; the effectively beneficent and happy man is accounted by a utilitarian more praiseworthy and admirable than any other type of man, and his useful life is thought the best kind of life than anyone could have, merely in virtue of its usefulness, and apart from any other characteristics it may have. The utilitarian philosophy picks out its own essential virtues very clearly, and the duties of a utilitarian are not hard to discern, even though they may on occasion involve difficult computations.

But there is one feature of familiar moralities which utilitarian ethics famously repudiates, or at least makes little of. There are a number of different moral prohibitions, apparent barriers to action, which a man acknowledges and which he thinks of as more or less insurmountable, except in abnormal, painful and improbable circumstances. One expects to meet these prohibitions, barriers to action, in certain quite distinct and clearly marked areas of action; these are the taking of human life, sexual relations, family duties and obligations, and the administration of justice according to the laws and customs of a given society. There are other areas in which strong barriers are to be expected; but these are, I think, the central and obvious ones. A morality is, at the very least, the regulation of the taking of life and the regulation of sexual relations, and it also includes rules of distributive and corrective justice: family duties: duties of friendship: also rights and duties in respect of money and property. When specific prohibitions in these areas are probed and challenged by reflection, and the rational grounds for them looked for, the questioner will think that he is questioning a particular morality specified by particular prohibitions. But if he were to question the validity of recognizing any prohibitions in these areas, he would think of himself as challenging the claims of morality itself; for the notion of morality requires that there be some strong barriers against the taking of life, against some varieties of sexual and family relations, against some forms of trial and punishment, some taking of property, and against some distributions of rewards and benefits.

Moral theories of the philosophical kind are differentiated in part by the different accounts that they give of these prohibitions: whether the prohibitions are to be thought of as systematically connected or not: whether they are absolute prohibitions or to be thought of as conditional. Utilitarians always had, and still have, very definite answers: first, they *are* systematically connected and, secondly, they are to be thought of as not absolute, but conditional, being dependent for their validity as prohibitions upon the beneficial consequences of observing them. Various reasons for rejecting the utilitarian position can be given.

All of us sometimes speak of things that cannot be done, or that must be done, and that are ruled out as impossible by the nature of the case: also there are things that one must do, that one cannot not do, because of the nature of the case. The signs of necessity in such contexts mark the unqualified, unweakened, barrier to action, while the word 'ought', too much discussed in philosophical writing, conveys a weakened prohibition or instruction. The same contrast appears in the context of empirical statements, as in the judgements 'The inflation ought to stop soon' and 'The inflation must stop soon.' The modal words 'must' and 'ought' preserve a constant relation in a number of different types of discourse, of which moral argument is only one, not particularly conspicuous, example: he who in a shop says to the salesman 'The coat must cover my knees', alternatively, 'The coat ought to cover my knees', speaks of a need or requirement and of something less: he who, looking at the mathematical puzzle, says 'This must be the way to solve it', alternatively 'This ought to be the way to solve it', speaks of a kind of rational necessity, and of something less: examples of 'ought' as the weaker variant of 'must' could be indefinitely prolonged into other types of contexts. So 'He must help him' is the basic, unmodified judgement in the context of moral discussion or reflection, and 'He ought to help him' is its weakened variant, as it is in other contexts.

The range of the utterly forbidden types of conduct in Victorian England would differ significantly, but not greatly, from the range of the forbidden and the impossible that would be acknowledged now. Social anthropologists may record fairly wide variations in the range of the morally impossible, and also, I believe, some barriers that are very general, though not quite universal; and historians similarly. For example, in addition to certain fairly specific types of killing, certain fairly specific types of sexual promiscuity, certain taking of property, there are also types of disloyalty and of cowardice, particularly disloyalty to friends, which are very generally, almost universally, forbidden and forbidden absolutely: they are forbidden as being intrinsically disgraceful and unworthy, and as being, just for these reasons, ruled out: ruled out because they would be disgusting, or disgraceful, or shameful, or brutal, or inhuman, or base, or an outrage.

In arguing against utilitarians I must dwell a little on these epithets usually associated with morally impossible action, on a sense of disgrace, of outrage, of horror, of baseness, of brutality, and, most important, a sense that a barrier, assumed to be firm and almost insurmountable, has been knocked over, and a feeling that, if this horrible, or outrageous, or squalid, or brutal, action is possible, then anything is possible and nothing is forbidden, and all restraints are threatened. Evidently these ideas have often been associated with impiety, and with a belief that God, or the Gods, have been defied, and with a fear of divine anger. But they need not have these associations with the supernatural, and they may have, and often have had, a secular setting. In the face of the doing of something that must not be done, and that is categorically excluded and forbidden morally, the fear that one may feel is fear of human nature. A relapse into a state of nature seems a real possibility: or perhaps seems actually to have occurred, unless an alternative morality with new restraints is clearly implied when the old barrier is crossed. This fear of human nature, and sense of outrage, when a barrier is broken down, is an aspect of respect for morality itself rather than for any particular morality and for any particular set of prohibitions. The notion of the morally impossible – 'I cannot leave him now: it would be quite impossible.' 'Surely you understand that I *must* help him' – is distinct. A course of conduct is ruled out ('You cannot do that'), because it would be inexcusably unjust, or dishonest, or humiliating, or treacherous, or cruel, or ungenerous, or harsh. These epithets, specifying why the conduct is impossible, mark the vices characteristically recognized in a particular morality. In other societies, at other places and times, other specific epithets might be more usually associated with outrage and morally impossible conduct; but the outrage or shock, and the recognition of impossibility, will be the same in cases where the type of conduct rejected, and the reasons for the rejection, are rather different.

The utilitarian will not deny these facts, but he will interpret them differently. Shock, he will say, is the primitive, pre-rational reaction; after rational reflection the strength of feeling associated with a prohibition can be, and ought to be, proportional to the estimated harm of the immediate and remote consequences; and he will find no more in the signs of necessity and impossibility than an emphasis on the moral rules which have proved to be necessary protections against evil effect. The signs of necessity are signs that there is a rule. But the rational justification of there being a rule is to be found in the full consequences of its observance, and not in non-rational reactions of horror, disgust, shame, and other emotional repugnances.

I believe that critical reflection may leave the notion of absolutely forbidden, because absolutely repugnant, conduct untouched. These may in many cases be good reflective reasons why doing such things, assuming such a character, may be abhorrent, and excluded from the range of possible conduct; there may be reflective reasons, in the sense that one is able to say why the conduct is impossible as destroying the ideal of a way of life that one aspires to and respects, as being, for example, utterly unjust or cruel or treacherous or corruptly dishonest. To show that these vices are vices, and unconditionally to be avoided, would take one back to the criteria for the assessment of persons as persons, and therefore to the whole way of life that one aspires to as the best way of life. A reflective, critical scrutiny of moral claims is compatible, both logically and psychologically, with an overriding concern for a record of unmonstrous and respect-worthy conduct, and of action that has never been mean or inhuman; and it may follow an assessment of the worth of persons which is not to be identified only with a computation of consequences and effects.

There is a model of rational reflection which depends upon a contrast between the primitive moral response of an uneducated man, and of an uneducated society, and the comparatively detached arguments of the sophisticated moralist who discounts his intuitive responses as being prejudices inherited from an uncritical past. Conspicuous in the philosophical radicals, in John Stuart Mill, and in the Victorian free-thinkers generally, this model in turn depended upon the idea that primitive, pre-scientific men are usually governed by strict moral taboos, an that in future intellectually-evolved, and scientifically trained, men will be emancipated from these bonds, and will start again with clear reasoning about consequences. The word 'taboo', so often used in these contexts, shows the assumption of moral progress from primitive beginnings, and suggests a rather naive contrast between older moralities and the open morality of the future; empirical calculation succeeds *a priori* prejudice, and the calculation of consequences is reason.

But reflection may discover a plurality of clear and definite moral injunctions; injunctions about the taking of life, about sexual relations, about the conduct of parents towards children and of children towards parents, about one's duties in times of war, about the conditions under which truth must be told and under which it may be concealed, about rights of property, about duties of friendship, and so on over the various aspects and phases of a normal span of life. Such injunctions need not be inferrable from a few basic principles, corresponding to the axioms of a theory. The pattern that they form can have a different type of unity. Taken together, a full set of such injunctions, prohibiting types of conduct in types of circumstance, decribes in rough and indeterminate outline, an attainable and recognizable way of life, aspired to, respected and admired: or at least the minimum general features of a respect-worthy way of life. And a way of life is not identified and characterized by one distinct purpose, such as the increase of general happiness, or even by a set of such distinct purposes. The connection between the injunctions, the connection upon which a reasonable man reflects, is to be found in the coherence of a single way of life, distinguished by the characteristic virtues and vices recognized within it.

A way of life is a complicated thing, marked out by many details of style and manner, and also by particular activities and interests, which a group of people of similar dispositions in a similar social situation may share; so that the group may become an imitable human type who transmit many of their habits and ideals to their descendants, provided that social change is not too rapid. In rational reflection one may justify an intuitively accepted and unconditional prohibition as a common, expected feature of a recognizable way of life which on other grounds one values and finds admirable: or as a necessary preliminary condition of this way of life. There are rather precise grounds in experience and in history for the reasonable man to expect that certain virtues, which he admires and values, can only be attained at the cost of certain others, and that the virtues typical of several different ways of life cannot be freely combined, as he might wish. Therefore a reasonable and reflective person will review the separate moral injunctions, which intuitively present themselves as having force and authority, as making a skeleton of an attainable, respectworthy and preferred way of life. He will reject those that seem likely in practice to conflict with others that seem more closely part of, or conditions of, the way of life that he values and admires, or that seem irrelevant to this way of life.

One must not exaggerate the degree of connectedness that can be claimed for the set of injuctions that constitute the skeleton of a man's morality. For example, it is a loose, empirical connection that reasonably associates certain sexual customs with the observation of certain family duties, and certain loyalties to the state or country with the recognition of certain duties in respect of property, and in time of war. The phrase 'way of life' is vague, and is chosen for its vagueness. The unity of a single way of life, and the compatibility in practice of different habits and dispositions, are learnt from observation, direct experience and from psychology and history; we know that human nature naturally varies, and is deliberately variable, only within limits; and that not all theoretically compatible achievements and enjoyments are compatible in normal circumstances. A reasonable man may envisage a way of life, which excludes various kinds of conduct as impossible, without excluding a great variety of morally tolerable ways of life within this minimum framework. The moral prohibitions constitute a kind of grammar of conduct, showing the elements out of which any fully respect-worthy conduct, as one conceives it, must be built.

The plurality of absolute prohibitions, and the looseness of their association with any one way of life, which stresses a certain set of virtues, is to be contrasted with the unity and simplicity of utilitarian ethics. One might interpret the contrast in this way: to the utilitarian it is certain that all reasonable purposes are parts of a single purpose in a creature known to be governed by the pleasure principle or by a variant of it. The anti-utilitarian replies: nothing is certain in the *theory* of morality: but, at a pre-theoretical level, some human virtues fit together as virtues to form a way of life aspired to, and some monstrous and brutal acts are certainly vicious in the sense that they undermine and corrupt this way of life; and we can explain why they are, and what makes them so, provided that we do not insist upon either precision or certainty or simplicity in the explanation.

The absolute moral prohibitions, which I am defending, are not to be identified with Kant's categorical moral injunctions; for they are not to be picked out by the logical feature of being universal in form. Nor are they prescriptions that must be affirmed, and that cannot be questioned or denied, just because they are principles of rationality, and because any contrary principles would involve a form of contradiction. They are indeed judgements of unconditional necessity, in the sense that they imply that what must be done is not necessary because it is a means to some independently valued end, but because the action is a necessary part of a way of life and ideal of conduct. The necessity resides in the nature of the action itself, as specified in the fully explicit moral judgement. The principal and proximate grounds for claiming that the action must, or must not, be performed are to be found in the characterization of the action offered within the prescription; and if the argument is pressed further, first a virtue or vice, and then a whole way of life will have to be described.

But still a number of distinctions are needed to avoid misunderstandings. First, he who says, for example, 'You must not give a judgement about this until you have heard the evidence', or 'I must stand by my friend in this crisis', claiming an absolute, and unconditional, necessity to act just so on this occasion, is not claiming an overriding necessity so to act in all circumstances and situations. He has so far not generalized at all, as he would have generalized if he were to add 'always' or 'in all circumstances'. The immediate grounds for the necessity of the action or abstention are indicated in the judgement itself. These particular actions, which are cases of the general type 'respecting evidence' and 'standing by friends', are said to be necessary on this occasion in virtue of having just this character, and in virtue of their being this type of action. In other painful circumstances, and on other occasions, other unconditional necessities, with other grounds, might possibly be judged to have overriding claims.

In a situation of conflict, two necessities may be felt to be stringent, and even generally inescapable, and the agent's further reflection may confirm his first feeling of their stringency. Yet in the circumstances of conflict he has to make a choice, and to bring himself to do one of the normally forbidden things, in order to avoid doing the other. He may finally recognize one overriding necessity, even though he would not be ready to generalize it to other circumstances. The necessity that is associated with types of action – for example, not to betray one's friends – is absolute and unconditional, in the sense that it is not relative to, or conditional upon, some desirable external end; but it is exposed exceptionally to conflict with other necessities.

A second distinction must be drawn: from the fact that a man thinks that there is nothing other than *X* which he can decently do in a particular situation it does not follow that it is intuitively obvious to him that he must do *X*. Certainly he may have reached the conclusion immediately and without reflection; but he might also have reached the very same conclusion after weighing a number of arguments for and against. A person's belief that so-and-so must be done, and that he must not act in any other way, may be the outcome of the calculation of the consequences of not doing the necessary thing: always provided that he sees the avoidance of bringing about these consequences as something that is imposed on him as a necessity in virtue of the character of the situation. The reason for the necessity of the action sometimes is to be found in its later consequences, rather than in the nature and quality of the action evident at the time of action. In every case there will be a description of the action that shows the immediate ground for the necessity, usually by indicating the virtue or vice involved.

Different men, and different social groups, recognize rather different moral necessities in the same essential areas of moral concern. This is no more surprising, or philosophically disquieting, than the fact that different men, and different social groups, will order the primary virtues of men, and the features of an admirable way of life, differently. That the poverty-stricken and the destitute must be helped, just because they suffer, and that a great wrong does not demand a great punishment as retribution, are typical modern opinions about what must be done. Reasoning is associated with these opinions, as it is also with the different orderings of essential virtues; there are no conclusive proofs, or infallible intuitions, which put a stop to the adducing of new considerations. One does not expect that everyone should recognize the same moral necessities; but rather that everyone should recognize some moral necessities, and similar and overlapping ones, in the same, or almost the same areas, of moral concern.

A person's morality, and the morality of a social group, can properly be seen as falling into two parts, first, a picture of the activities necessary to an ideal way of life which is aspired to, and, secondly, the unavoidable duties and necessities without which even the elements of human worth, and of a respect-worthy way of life, are lacking. The two parts are not rationally unconnected. To take the obvious, classical examples: a betrayal of friends in a moment of danger, and for the sake of one's own safety, is excluded from the calculation of possibilities; one may lose perhaps everything else, but this cannot be done; the stain would be too great. And one may take public examples: an outrage of cruelty perpetrated upon undefended civilians in war would constitute a stain that would not be erased and would not be balanced against political success.

How would a rational disciple of Sidgwick, a philosophical friend of the utilitarians, respond to these suggestions? Among other objections he would certainly say that I was turning the clock back, suggesting a return to the moral philosophies of the past: absolute prohibitions, elementary decencies, the recognition of a plurality of prohibitions which do not all serve a single purpose: and with nothing more definite behind them than a form of life aspired to; this is the outline of an Aristotelian ethics: ancient doctrine. Modern utilitarians thought that people have the possibility of indefinite improvement in their moral thinking, and that they were confined and confused by their innate endowments of moral repugnances and emotional admirations. There was a sense of the open future in all their writing. But hope of continuing improvement, if it survives at all now, is now largely without evidence. Lowering the barriers of prohibition, and making rational calculation of consequences the sole foundation of public policies, have so far favoured, and are still favouring, a new callousness in policy, a dullness of sensibility, and sometimes moral despair, at least in respect of public affairs. When the generally respected barriers of impermissible conduct are once crossed, and when no different unconditional barriers, within the same areas of conduct, are put in their place, then the special, apparently superstitious, value attached to the preservation of human life will be questioned. This particular value will no longer be distinguished by an exceptionally solemn prohibition; rather it will be assessed on a common scale alongside other desirable things. Yet it is not clear that the taking of lives can be marked and evaluated on a common scale on which increases of pleasure and diminutions of suffering are also measured. This is the suggested discontinuity which a utilitarian must deny.

Moral prohibitions in general, and particularly those that govern the taking of life, the celebration of the dead, and that govern sexual relations and family relations, are artifices that give human lives some distinctive, peculiar, even arbitrary human shape and pattern. They humanize the natural phases of experience, and lend them a distinguishing sense and direction, one among many possible ones. It is natural for men to expect these artificialities, without which their lives would seem to them inhuman. Largely for this reason a purely naturalistic and utilitarian interpretation of duties and obligations, permissions and prohibitions, in these areas, and particularly in the taking of human life, leaves uneasiness. The idea of morality is historically connected with the idea that taking human life is a terrible act, which has to be regulated by some set of overriding constraints that constitute a morality; and the connection of ideas alleged here is not a vague one. If there were a people who did not recoil from killing, and, what is a distinguishable matter, who seemed to attach no exceptional value to human life, they would be accounted a community of the sub-human; or, more probably, we would doubt whether their words and practices had been rightly interpreted and whether their way of life had been understood. Yet the taking of life does not have any exceptional importance in utilitarian ethics; the taking of life is morally significant in so far as it brings other losses with it. For a strict utilitarian the horror of killing is only the horror of causing other losses, principally of possible happiness; in cases where there are evidently no such losses, the horror of killing becomes superstition. And such a conclusion of naturalism, pressed to its limits, does produce a certain vertigo after reflection. It seems that a main source of morality has been taken away.

This vertigo is not principally the result of looking across a century of cool political massacres, undertaken with rational aims; it is also a sentiment with a philosophical thought behind it: A consistent naturalism displaces the pre-reflective moral emphasis upon respect for life, and for the preservation of life, on to an exclusive concern for one or other of the expected future products of being alive – happiness, pleasure, the satisfaction of desires. Respect for human life, independent of the use made of it, may seem to utilitarians a survival of a sacramental consciousness, or at least a survival of a doctrine of the soul's destiny, or of the unique relation between God and man. It had been natural to speak of the sacred prohibitions against the taking of life; and this phrase has no proper place, it is very reasonably assumed, in the thought of anyone who has rejected belief in supernatural sanctions.

The situation may be more complicated. The sacredness of life, so called, and the absolute prohibitions against the taking of life, except under strictly defined conditions, may be admitted to be human inventions. Once the human origin of the prohibitions has been recognized, the prohibition against the taking of life, and respect for human life as such, may still be reaffirmed as absolute. They are reaffirmed as complementary to a set of customs and observances, which are sometimes understood by reference to their function, and which are sustained, partly because of, partly in spite of, this understanding: I mean sexual customs, family observances, ceremonial treatment of the dead, gentle treatment of those who are diseased and useless, and of the old and senile, customs of war and treatment of prisoners, treatment of convicted criminals, political and legal safeguards for the rights of individuals, and the customary rights of respect and gentleness in personal dealings. This complex of habits, and the rituals associated with them, are carried over into a secular morality which makes no existential claims that a naturalist would dispute, and which still rejects the utilitarian morality associated with naturalism. The error of the optimistic utilitarian is that he carries the deritualization of transactions between men to a point at which men not only can, but ought to, use and exploit each other as they use and exploit any other natural objects, as far as this is compatible with general happiness. And at this point, when the mere existence of an individual person by itself has no value, apart from the by-products and uses of the individual in producing and enjoying desirable states of mind, there is no theoretical barrier against social surgery of all kinds. Not only is there no such barrier in theory: but, more important, the non-existence of the barriers is explicitly recognized. The draining of moral significance from ceremonies, rituals, manners and observances, which imaginatively express moral attitudes and prohibitions, leaves morality incorporated only in a set of propositions and computations: thin and uninteresting propositions, when so isolated from their base in the observances, and the manners, which govern ordinary relations with people, and which always manifest implicit moral attitudes and opinions. The computational morality, on which optimists rely, dismisses the non-propositional and unprogrammed elements in morality altogether, falsely confident that these elements can all be ticketed and brought into the computations.

I now seem to be arguing for the truth of a doctrine by pointing to the evil consequences of its being disbelieved: this is not my meaning. I have been assuming that prohibitions against killing are primary moral prohibitions; secondly, that the customs and rituals that govern, in different societies, relations between the sexes, marriage, property rights, family relationships, and the celebration of the dead, are primary moral customs; they always disclose the peculiar kind of respect for human life, and occasions for disrespect, which a particular people or society recognizes, and therefore their more fundamental moral beliefs and attitudes. Ordinarily a cosmology, or metaphysics, is associated with the morality, and, for Europeans, it has usually been a supernatural cosmology. When the supernatural cosmology is generally rejected, or no longer is taken seriously, the idea that human life has a unique value has to be recognized as a human invention. But it is not an invention from nothing at all; the rituals and manners that govern behaviour and respect for persons already express a complex set of moral beliefs and attitudes, and embody a particular way of life. Affirmations of particular rights, duties and obligations, the propositions of a morality, are a development and a correction of this inexplicit morality of ritual and manners.

Each society, each generation within it, and, in the last resort, each reflective individual, accepts and amends an established morality expressed in rituals and manners, and in explicit prohibitions; and he will do this, in determining what kind of person he aspires to be and what are the necessary features of a desirable and admirable way of life as he conceives it. If these prohibitions, whatever they are, were no longer observed, and the particular way of life, which depends on them, was lost, and not just amended or replaced, no particular reason would be left to protect human life more than any other natural phenomenon. The different manners of different societies provide, as an element in good manners, for the recognition of differences; so among the more serious moral constraints – serious in the sense that they regulate killing and sexuality and family relationships, and so the conditions of survival of the species – may be the requirement to respect moral differences, at least in certain cases. Provided that there are absolute prohibitions in the same domains with the same function, and provided that their congruence with a desired way of life is grasped, we may without irrationality accept the differences; and there may sometimes be a duty to avoid conflict or to look for compromise in cases of conflict. Consider the intermediate case between manners in the restricted sense and absolute moral principles: a code of honour of a traditional kind. The different prohibitions of different codes are still recognized as codes of honour; and dishonour incurred in the breach of different disciplines is in each case recognizably dishonour, in virtue of the type of ideal behaviour, and the way of life, that has been betrayed. Prohibitions in other moralities, very different from the moralities of honour, may be similarly diverse in content.

The question cannot be evaded: what is the rational basis for acting as if human life has a peculiar value, quite beyond the value of any other natural things, when one can understand so clearly how different people, for quite different reasons, have come to believe that it has a particular value and to affirm this in their different moralities? Is one not rationally compelled to follow the utilitarians in denying the autonomy of ethics, and the absoluteness of moral prohibitions, if once one comes to understand the social, psychological and other functions which the prohibitions serve? If one reflectively adopts and reaffirms one or other of these moralities, together with its prohibitions, then it may seem that one must be accepting the morality for the sake of its uses and function, rather than for the other reasoning associated with it; and this concedes the utilitarians' case.

The conclusion is not necessary. A morality, with its ordering of virtues and its prohibitions, provides a particular ideal of humanity in an ideal way of life; and this moral ideal explains where and why killing is allowed and also for what purpose a man might reasonably give his life; and in this sense it sets its own peculiar value on human life. One cannot doubt that there are causes, largely unknown, that would explain why one particular ideal has a hold upon people at a particular time and place, apart from the reasoning that they would use to defend it. And it seems certain that the repugnances and horror surrounding some moral prohibitions are sentiments that have both a biological and a social function. But the attitude of a reflective person to these repugnances and prohibitions does not for this reason have to be a utilitarian one. One may on reflection respect and reaffirm the prohibitions, and the way of life that they protect, for reasons unconnected with their known or presumed functions. The reasons that lead a reflective person to prefer one code of manners, or one legal system, to another must be moral reasons; that is, he must find his reasons in some order of priority of interests and activities in the kind of life that he praises and admires and that he aspired to have, and in the kind of person that he wants to become. Reasons for the most general moral choices, which may sometimes be choices among competing moralities, must be found in philosophical reasoning, if they are found at all: that is, in considerations about the relation of persons to the natural, or to the supernatural, order.

I shall mention one inclining philosophical reason, which has in the past been prominent in moral theories, particularly those of Aristotle and of Spinoza, and which influences me. One may on reflection find a particular set of prohibitions and injunctions, and a particular way of life protected by them, acceptable and respect-worthy, partly because this specifically conceived way of life, with its accompanying prohibitions, has in history appeared natural, and on the whole still feels natural, both to oneself and to others. If there are no overriding reasons for rejecting this way of life, or for rejecting some distinguising features of it, its felt and proven naturalness is one reason among others for accepting it. This reason is likely to influence particularly those who, unlike utilitarians, cannot for other reasons believe that specific states of mind of human beings are the only elements of value in the universe: who, on the contrary, believe that the natural order as a whole is the fitting object of that kind of unconditional interest and respect that is called moral: that the peculiar value to be attached to human life, and the prohibitions against the taking of human life, are not dependent on regarding and treating human beings as radically different from other species in having some supernatural destiny: that the exceptional value attached both to individual lives, and to the survival of the species as a whole, resides in the power of the human mind to begin to understand, and to enjoy, the natural order as a whole, and to reflect upon this understanding and enjoyment: and that, apart from this exceptional power, the uncompensated destruction of any species is always a loss to be avoided.

In the previous century George Eliot and George Henry Lewes had accepted a variant of Spinozistic naturalism close to the doctrine that I have been suggesting. But they still believed in the probability of future moral improvements, once superstitions had gone. Their ethics was still imbued with an optimism that was certainly not shared by Spinoza, and with a sense of an open and unconfined future for the species. Spinoza's own naturalism was quite free from optimism about the historical future. He did not suggest that advanced, highly educated societies will for the first time be governed largely by the dictates of reason, and that human nature will radically change, and that the conflict between reason and the incapacitating emotions will be largely resolved. Rather he suggests an opposing view of history and of the future: that moral progress, in the proper sense of the increasing dominance of gentleness and of reason, is not to be expected except within very narrow limits. He thought that he knew that, as psycho-physical organisms, persons are so constructed that there must always in most men and women be recurrences of unreason alongside reason, and that in this respect social and historical change would be superficial in their consequences. This pessimism, or at least lack of optimism, is compatible with a secular doctrine, akin to that of natural law, which represents many of the seemingly natural prohibitions of non-computational morality as more likely to be endorsed than to be superseded by reflection. A naturalist of his persuasion does not foresee a future in which rational computation will by itself replace the various imaginations, unconscious memories and habits, rituals and manners, which have lent substance and content to men's moral ideas, and which have partly formed their various ways of life.

Some of these ways of life, and certainly their complexity and variety, may be respected as an aspect of natural variety: and, like other natural phenomena, they may over the years be studied and explained, at least to some degree explained. From this point of view, that of natural knowledge, the species, if it survives, may perhaps make interesting advances. But this was not the utilitarians' hope; they looked for an historical transformation of human nature, through new moral reasoning, and this has not occurred and is now not to be reasonably expected.

5

Public and Private Morality

1

In chapter 4 I have used the phrase 'rational computational morality' in a pejorative sense, and I write about the abstract cruelty in politics which had been associated in the USA during the Vietnam War with a new quasi-quantitative precision in the calculation of the consequences of alternative policies. These charges against a type of utilitarian thinking need fully argued support, and particularly the use of 'rational' here and of 'abstract' needs to be explained. Why should 'rational' be used in an abusive sense? It was perhaps evident that I was drawing on an Aristotelian idea of the form of rationality which is involved in practical reasoning. There is a presumed distinction between rationality in choosing between lines of conduct, practical reason, and rationality in arriving at true statements and beliefs, theoretical reason; and this distinction is associated with a specific account of practical reasoning. Within this account the word 'abstract', when applied to practical reasoning, becomes a reproach and for several distinct reasons. Even the word 'rational', as it occurs in the phrase 'rational computational morality', can be part of a reproach, because of the implication that the wrong model of rationality is involved: wrong, in the sense that it is inappropriate to much practical reasoning, even if it is appropriate to reasoning of other kinds.

2

I shall borrow from Aristotle that emphasis on the normal condensation of practical reasoning which makes it resemble perception, or, more strictly, perceptual identification. I can tell that the aeroplane is a Dornier, and there is an answer to the question 'How did I tell?' The stages and steps in aircraft recognition will be brought to light when the activity is being taught to beginners in recognition. In the process of learning, the many stages and steps, at first taken deliberately and one by one, gradually become internalized and are finally not only unnoticed but practically unnoticeable. When the learning is finished and the performance fully internalized, the subject no longer even thinks of recognition as having stages and steps, unless he runs into difficulties, and not necessarily even then.

The reasoning that enters into perceptual identification, both of types and of individuals, is probably the commonest of all types of reasoning, and therefore the most thoroughly learnt and fully internalized. Aristotle makes the comparison between perceptual judgement, and the reasoning entering into it, and practical choice in substantial moral issues, and the reasoning entering into that, when he wants to stress the internalization of norms of conduct in the experienced man of settled dispositions. It is evidently a partial parallel, but it holds for Aristotle's limited purposes. It may be supplemented by parallels with other cases of condensed reasoning which are closer to the reasoning that enters into moral judgement and into substantial moral decisions.

Consider the rules, conventions, and habits of behaviour which fall under the broad heading of manners, that is, social manners in any society and social group. Manners are apt to be:

(a) learnt both by precept and by example;
(b) finally habitual, unconsidered, and wholly internalized;
(c) applied in particular situations which are immediately recognized as falling under a certain convention-invoking description, and both this recognition, and also the choice of behaviour to which it leads, involve condensed reasoning. There is a fourth characteristic of the choice of behaviour to be noted;
(d) in difficult situations of conflict of conventions, or of rules, of good manners, in situations which are normally not too common, the subject has to make his choice of behaviour explicit to himself, and also to make explicit the reasoning which supports his conclusion.

Manners provide a close parallel to the morals of private life in the relation of implicit and explicit reasoning to conduct. Our patterns of behaviour, from infancy onwards, are permeated by explicitly learnt, and by imitated, rituals and set forms of address in more or less finely discriminated social situations and family situations. There is a large overlapping, even in modern societies, between the claims of good manners and moral claims.

We do normally have reasons for the modification of our behaviour in situations in accordance with accepted manners, even if we are totally unable to say what these reasons are, when we are asked; that is, 'He has a reason for behaving in such-and-such a manner in such-and-such situations' does not entail either 'He is now able to say why he behaves as he does', or even 'He would recognize the correct account of why he behaves as he does, if it were suggested to him.' He might have learnt, by imitating his elders, to adapt his behaviour to changing situations in accordance with rules and conventions which have never been explicitly stated to him, and even according to rules which have never been explicitly stated at all.

Suppose that he has learnt by imitation over a long period of time to adapt his posture and mode of address to fit the different sex, age and social standing of the persons whom he meets. When he makes a mistake, and behaves unfittingly, his mistake is described with the minimum of generality: for example, 'She is an old woman, and the wife of a relation of yours, so why did you behave so casually?' He has learnt his variations of behaviour in the same way that he learnt to speak his native language: by imitating others and by being corrected, with greater or less generality, when he goes wrong. He need not have learnt a code of manners, explicitly formulated, any more than he need have learnt the rules of grammar applicable to his native tongue. In both cases one could speak of the rules and conventions being internalized.

I have chosen as an example manners to compare with morality, in respect of internalized rules and conventions, because manners are near to morals on the one side and akin to language on the other side. It is generally held to be a positive advantage that manners should be internalized, and that a man should not need to consult a remembered code-book, or a set of instructions, in order to be sure how he should behave in various situations. Manners should be 'natural', it is said, or should be 'instinctive'. The implication is that the correct behaviour should not be the outcome of careful and laborious calculation and reflection; it should be immediate, spontaneous, governed by intuition. Something similar would be claimed for the proper command of a language; one should be able to speak spontaneously and intuitively, and to select the right word without reflection and without recourse to dictionary or grammar. Also the swift and intuitive choice of the right words is often a matter of good manners and sometimes also a moral matter; for instance, as clearly expressing the right feeling.

Aristotle allowed very little difference in this respect between morality and good manners. Both should be fully internalized as stable dispositions which lead, effortlessly and immediately, to reasonable conduct and to reasonable assessments of situations demanding action, and to making the assessments without too much brooding and effort. He specifically compares acting from a stable disposition with the effortless correct use of language; it is not sufficient to do what the grammatical man does. One must do it in the same way.

Is there, and must there be, a difference between manners and morals in this one specific respect: that the rules of good manners, generally speaking, are, among other things, necessarily internalized, and, in this sense, should become natural, while no such implication holds for the rational man whose conduct, in politics or private life, is morally admirable? Is this a valid contrast? As soon as the question is posed, it is evident that different moral theories yield different answers to the question and that our pre-theoretical intuitions are not decisive. Aristotelian theory entails that there is no very significant difference between manners and morals in this respect, and this is part of the reason, within the theory, why there is for him no ultimate divergence in the normal run of things between a morally admirable life and a satisfying and happy one; for to the person who is rational in substantial practical matters it has become second nature to act rightly and he does so more or less effortlessly and as a matter of course and with pleasure. The most significant advantages of explicitness in moral reasoning are that explicit knowledge of the reasons why (a) is in itself an intellectual virtue, and (b) explicit knowledge of the reasons why is necessary for the person who takes a leading part in public life and in affairs of state. He has to explain and recommend his policies to others. (c) Explicit reasoning is more open to being checked and confusions in reasoning are in general more likely to be noticed.

There is no implication within Kantian theory that the imperatives which practical reason must follow are internalized except in the person of holy will; and there is certainly no implication that the imperatives of morality are to be compared with, or essentially resemble, the imperatives of a code of manners. The implication is very much the reverse: good manners require accurate discrimination between variously different social situations in a minutely observant spirit, and they do not require high-level generalizations.

The contrast can be represented as that between noticing a great number and variety of independently variable features of particular situations on the one hand, and on the other hand bringing a few, wholly explicit principles to bear upon situations, which have to be subsumed under the principles, as in some kinds of legal reasoning. Kant was assimilating important practical reasoning and decision-making to laying down the law, rather as God lays down the law. Aristotle assimilated political decision-making, and practical reasoning generally, to the condensed, trained judgement of particular situations by games-players, craftsmen, performers of all kinds. Evidently these are assimilations only, not claimed identities; but the difference between the assimilations is significant. Different models of rationality in practical reasoning are implied by the assimilations.

Like the rules and conventions of language, the rules and conventions of good manners need to be codified, or at least to be well understood, because they govern transactions between persons and they require conformity in response. The responses need to be, in the most strict sense, regular and expected. There is advantage in their being habitual, and in their being inbuilt, reliable dispositions; the less brooding on difficult cases the better for social ease and harmony. More fundamentally, codes of manners, like languages, are essentially various, serving to distinguish different social groups. Any one social group may in fact believe that its good manners are the only good manners, and that its good manners ought ideally to be recognized by all groups as constituting good manners. Anyone who seriously makes this claim, and who supports it with argument, and who argues that other conceptions of good manners are in some way mistaken or inferior, is in effect claiming that his good manners are a proper part of morality. He has crossed the uncertain frontier between manners and morality, as they are now recognized, when he makes the claim that there is a good reason why everyone ought to behave as his particular norm of good manners precribes, whether these are the manners of a man's social group or not. If there is a right way to behave to which all men are required to conform, and if there is some coherent reason why this behaviour is required of all men, it is difficult to see how the label 'moral' could be withheld from this requirement.

3

Does right conduct in public and private life alike, and judged from a serious moral point of view, constantly require explicit thought, and the careful weighing of arguments, and the making of calculations? Most utilitarian moralists will say that rationality in practical reasoning, where serious moral issues are concerned, is incompatible with habitual responses and internalized dispositions; in the context of practical reason on moral issues, rationality entails constant calculation, and specifically calculation of consequences. This calculation may be performed rapidly and habitually, but always the calculation can be, and ought to be, reconstructed and made explicit. This is the position that must be examined. Is it a necessary condition of a man being rational in his practical decisions that he should be able, in some appropriate setting, to give a satisfactory account of his reasons? Shall we have to say, in a serious moral case, that his decision was irrational, in a bad sense, if he is unable to explain his decision as the conclusion of a calculation, and of a calculation that is respectable? The Aristotelian analogy with perception is used to suggest that it does not follow from the fact that a man does not know what his reasons were for a decision just taken that there were no good reasons, and that he acted under the influence of causes that do not count as reasons; for instance, that he acted without thought or impulsively, or as an unthinking response to some stimulus, or because he just wanted to, when the desire was an unthinking one. It is not essential to being a reason that the thought that constitutes a reason should be accessible, under favourable conditions, to the consciousness of the thinker and agent.

The principal argument for this conclusion starts from a philosophical premise, which in *Thought and Action* I dubbed the inexhaustibility of description. Any situation which confronts me, and which is not a situation in a game, has an inexhaustible set of discriminable features over and above those which I explicitly notice at the time because they are of immediate interest to me. Secondly, the situation has features over and above those which are mentionable within the vocabulary that I possess and use. I 'take in' the situation, noticing the features that are particularly relevant to my interests at the time, and I respond to it in accordance with my prevailing desires and purposes and my prevailing beliefs and knowledge about the means to satisfy them. The reasons for my actions and conduct, when the actions are voluntary and intended, are to be found in my contemporary desires, current or standing, in my beliefs and knowledge, taken together. My desires and interests form a vast system, and only a few of them are called into play at any one time. Of many of them I would not know how strong they were, or even that they existed, until some situation requiring carefully considered action brings them to my attention. Only a very few of them are desires formed after reflection and therefore explicitly recognized at their birth. As for the system of my beliefs, it is evident that there is in my mind a vast store of unsurveyable background knowledge and belief; and against this background my specific beliefs about the present situation form themselves.

When it comes to giving an account of the reasons for an action, or course of conduct, one picks out a few salient desires and beliefs from the foreground of consciousness and, more specifically, those that distinguish this particular occasion and this particular person: the ordinary, run-of-the-mill desires and beliefs are not worth mentioning. Even in the case of action following upon fully explicit deliberation, and of a contemporary account of the reasons for the decision, the reasons are a selection of the interesting items, and are recognized as being a selection.

The parallel with language is useful. It has so far proved impossible to design a translating machine which takes account of the indefinite variety of contexts, linguistic and external, in which a given form of words is used; and normally the contexts affect the sense. However elaborate the programme built into the machine, it is apt to fall short, if only because of the sheer unpredictable variety of contexts encountered. The variety is not only humanly unpredictable but humanly unimaginable. Yet a person translating immediately sees the recurring form of words against the background of a different context and then intuitively makes the required adjustment to the sense. A person is a complex mechanism naturally designed over a long evolutionary period to make such adjustments.

For every choice of words that a translator makes in a particular context while translating, there is a complex of reasons, good or bad, which might account for the choice made; reasons drawn from the context, from the associations of the words remembered from the past, from the syntax of the speaker or writer, and so forth. A very experienced and successful translator might be unable to give the reasons that had led him to choose one word as the appropriate translation rather than another which is nearly synonymous. But he might be quite sure that there were reasons for the choice, which were his reasons, and that the choice was not an unthinking one. If he did reflect on the reasons for his choice, trying to evaluate them, he would normally have at least the following difficulties: the reasons that he gives would be the salient contexts, selected parallel passages and associations, picked out from the unrecoverable complex of his verbal memories of uses of these and of similar words. On reflection these selected contexts seem to him to have been present to his mind and in the foreground of his awareness, but against a huge background of other contexts and associations determining his decision, but not now recalled. He has no method, even in principle, of individuating the reasons determining his decision, and therefore of arriving at any exact causal statement, or any complete one. He could not remember the great number of obvious and undistinguished contexts in which he has encountered the words in question and which have finally given him a 'feeling', as one might say, for the possible standard employments of the words.

The skill in translating of a person who knows two languages well resides in a great accumulation of pre-conscious memories. That the memories should be pre-conscious, or unconscious, is a natural advantage because speed and fluency are of the essence of linguistic skills. There is little advantage for a translator in possessing the rather different skill which would be involved in giving an adequate account of the distinct reasons for his choice of equivalents. This advantage would exist if in normal circumstances a public defence of the decisions was required, and if the translations had to be publicly justified, before they could be accepted as adequate translations. Even in those imaginary circumstances the justification would fall short of being complete, for the reasons already given, and there would be residuary appeals to particular forms of words 'sounding right', also to associations of words which cannot be precisely distinguished and listed. The reason-giving would generally tail off into mere intuition, with claims of 'not sounding the same' and of 'seeming to fit'; and there would be appeals to the translator's accumulation of linguistic experience as in itself a kind of reason for accepting his decision as correct.

The analogy between decisions in translating from language to language, and the intuitions of rightness involved, and on the other side decisions about the right conduct in a situation requiring judgement is, first, an analogy in respect of multiplicity of uncountable background features normally involved in the deciding mind; secondly, in respect of the mind's ability, in sophisticated actions as in routine movements, to draw upon a vast store of memories which are pre-conscious; thirdly, in respect of the thinking that is in both cases highly condensed, and that is not for this reason to be reconstructed easily, as amounting to arguments which could be used in conclusive support of the decisions.

The skilled use of language is an extreme case of condensed and unreconstructible thinking, and our thinking about political and moral issues neither normally is, nor normally ought to be, to the same degree condensed and unreconstructible. Emotions lead to confusions in moral reasoning and a measure of explicitness is to some degree a safeguard against confusion so caused. But the extreme case of the translator's skill in choice of words illustrates that element in practical thinking on serious moral issues which a 'computational morality' either ignores or means to banish. The need for a reconstruction of the reasons for a decision, and for using that reconstruction as a part of a justification of the decision, is often to be expected where serious moral issues are confronted; and for this reason alone the analogy with language cannot be pressed too far. There is a difference of degree. But the analogy with law, which is usually invoked to illuminate reasoning about moral questions, also cannot be pressed too far in the opposite direction. The thought that enters into a legal decision must always be reconstructible as a potential argument in further justification of that decision. There must also be a known record of earlier relevant cases and decisions, and not a confused memory of an indefinite multiplicity of parallel cases.

That in the absence of difficulty and uncertainty, and when there is no discussion between persons, reasoning about conduct should be normally unreflective and implicit is an obvious advantage to the species. Over much of its range practical reason has to replace the largely inflexible and the largely predetermined responses and routines of animal behaviour. We have to think fast in the exercise of many skills which involve feeling and good judgement. Often we must not spend too much energy on reflection, where love and friendship are at risk.

What is the philosophical importance of this fact of the internalization of thinking processes? Why is it worth while to dwell on it, and to underline it? Part of the answer is: because there is a philosophical tradition which identifies the ideal of rationality with explicitness in moving from reasons to conclusions; and it is a very respectable tradition, traceable to Plato. Undeniably there are good reasons for associating rationality, as an ideal to be aimed at, with some degree of explicitness in moving from reasons to conclusions in difficult cases, and when justice and public policies are in question. But rationality ought not to be identified with explicitness.

The tradition is that to know why the moral claims that seem to us intuitively right are really right is to be able to show that they form a coherent system. Then the moral claims have the backing of reason, while our intuitions may be coloured by variable sentiments. After the discovery of coherence the moral claims are more secure, in a psychological sense, than they were before; that is the first advantage. The second traditional advantage is that some intuitions are rightly corrected when the stabilizing theory is fully understood; doubtful cases of moral claims are clarified and classified clearly within the theory, and conflict between claims are rendered intelligible by the theory, which explains why the conflicts must arise and how they are to be solved. Without the theory there is no clear method of distinguishing between a moral claim and a prejudice or superstition, and of isolating a mere effect of custom and habit. The theory must accord with the main run of moral claims which are recognized as binding, and it will at the same time explain why a few claims have come to seem binding, which, when examined systematically, are seen not to be. This is one traditional view of the value of moral theory. It associates rationality in moral judgement with coherence, which in turn implies an absence of irresoluble conflicts between moral claims. Rationality has exactly the same sense, and the same application, as in theoretical inquiries; the theory that guides the beliefs of the rational person should exclude unresolved conflicts between claims and should be comprehensive, covering all types of contingency. On the other hand intuitions, however carefully reflected upon, may at any time lead to irresoluble conflicts in practical judgement, prescribing two incompatible courses of conduct as necessary and as required of any morally respect-worthy person.

Science and law require as institutions public and argumentative justifications and a publicly defensible consistency. Irresoluble conflicts and incompatibility cannot be tolerated; not only that, but there is a requirement of a general and recognized method for resolving any apparently irresoluble conflicts and contradictions that arise. Consequently anyone thinking, alone and silently, about a scientific or a legal problem is thinking about the reasons he would give, if challenged, for any particular conclusion which his intuitions suggest is correct. He would not even allow his intuitive judgement to constitute his conclusions unless he could formulate, at least in outline, the reasons that he would cite in public argument; and the reasons would show the coherence of the judgement in question with a set of already accepted propositions. The private thought, the silent deliberation, take place under the shadow of the public institution.

If there is no shadow of the public and institutional test of a type of conclusion, and if a person is deeply concerned with the particular case before him and in being careful in his conclusion about it; if he is thinking alone, and if he is not particularly interested in proving to others that he has the right solution; under these conditions, the concept of rationality that is tied to giving satisfactory reasons will have a weaker hold on him. He will not be compelled, by the very nature of his interest, to be sure that any conclusion that he reaches is supported by sufficient reasons and that he has a convincing argument ready, if he is challenged. He will not necessarily need to make his inferences explicit, though he may wish to do so for reasons of his own, unconnected with public institutions. He may want to check that he has not 'leapt to a conclusion', following some association of ideas: to check that he is not believing his conclusion principally because he wants to believe it. A connoisseur attributes works of art to their right sources and infers their dates. He detects fakes, copies, the works of disciples and followers. He knows the real thing, lots of different kinds of real thing, within the range of his experience and study; but he is not usually able to say how he tells. Connoisseurs in countless other fields, apart from works of art, are in the same position; able to discriminate with consistent success, but not knowing at all precisely how they do it, not knowing what makes them arrive at the conclusion, usually the right one; having no explicitly formulated method which they are applying with any consciousness of what it is. They know that, like the translator, they are guided by a weight of experience of many similar cases and by many associations and memories, not all of which they can disentangle and recall. The memories are too extensive to be accessible, but methodically stored and linked by a causality which they do not understand and which is too complex to trace. The connoisseur – of drawings, of horses, of wines, of the wind and weather at sea – needs to concentrate on noticing unexpected features and on using his senses and on being open to impressions, and on being receptive to unexpected inputs, which may change his judgement. Negatively, he must not impose a ready-made rational structure on his observations, if this entails attending to ordinarily expected features of the object, and attending only with set ideas of what is relevant.

The connoisseur may never know, and be able to distinguish, the separate steps, or the separate inputs, which led him to his conclusion, and he may never be able to put his inference into any standard form. Another example – the inferences that lead one to understand the sentences of one's own language spoken by a foreigner in a strange accent are very complex and very efficient; but there would usually be no way of reconstructing the inferences that led to the conclusion in a standard order.

4

On what grounds do I argue that, in decisions of substantial moral concern, inferences of the intuitive kind have a proper place alongside inferences of the explicit and fully articulated kind? That we ought sometimes, even in serious issues of public policy, to follow our intuitions of what is best to be done, in spite of the fact that in some cases we cannot specify a convincing set of reasons to support the intuitions?

A defender of rationality in practical reasoning, in the traditional sense of 'rational', may admit that it is often difficult, and sometimes impossible, to make fully explicit the reasons for a decision made in a substantial moral issue. But he may argue that one ought to aim at full explicitness in specifying the principal reasons for a judgement in any serious moral issue, even if one does not succeed in disentangling every separate consideration that influenced the outcome. Following Aristotle, this defender of rationality of the traditional kind will argue that the policy of evaluating explicitly every consideration influencing him is a guarantee against confusions about the ends of action, misleading associations, subjective impressions, sentimental prejudice and superstition; and this is a sufficient vindication of traditional rationality in moral reasoning, quite apart from the occasional necessity of publicly defending a decision. The more careful and methodical the deliberation before action, with an explicit reviewing of arguments and counter-arguments, the less likely a man is to be misled by received opinions and mere confusions of thought.

To summarize the arguments in reply: the mind is an instrument developed by natural selection to identify objects, to learn and to speak languages, to perform an immense range of routine actions, to recognize and to respond appropriately and with feeling to persons and to form attachments to them, and to enter into all the interchanges of social life. It is also an instrument for abstract thought, and, more specifically, for learning mathematics and for grasping legal distinctions. In the abusive phrase 'abstract computational morality' the word 'abstract' is there for good reason. An abstraction has its natural and proper place in reasoning; so does its contrary, which is the mind's openness to a great range of largely unexpected observed features of a situation all of which are allowed to influence the response. Kant's account of practical reason was an insistence on the abstract will, which in virtue of its rationality would not be engaged by the multiplicity of concrete features that complicate particular situations. In virtue of its rationality Kant's practical reason, at least in serious moral issues, will conceive situations abstractly with a view to subsuming them under the relevant moral principle.

The opposing school of moralists, utilitarians, associate rationality in moral reasoning with scientific method, therefore with verifiable judgements of right and wrong, and therefore with a general criterion or test that yields definite results in particular cases. Therefore a primary abstraction is required, as in any applied science, an abstraction that leaves out of account in practical deliberation those features of situations which are not mentioned in the utilitarian calculus. The agent can feel secure with his rational method. He has eliminated the worst uncertainties of living and he is left with manageable empirical calculations; and these are the kind of calculation which every prudent and efficient man makes every day, fitting accessible means to desired ends. Much that is puzzling, exceptional and difficult about those practical questions which are called moral issues has been cleared away for the utilitarian by a policy of abstraction.

5

If I were to defend further the case against abstract thinking in many matters of moral judgement, and against abstract thinking in the conduct of public affairs, I would do best to tell true stories, drawn from direct experience, of events which have actually involved difficult decisions. Some of the decisions would be matters of public policy, and the agent would have a public and a representative role complicating the decision for him. Some of the decisions would arise from tangled situations in private life, and the story would need to describe fully and carefully the dispositions and feelings and history of the persons involved. Telling the stories, with the facts taken from experience and not filleted and at second hand, imposes some principles of selection. One has to decide what the story is and what the situation is, or was, from the point of view of morality. In telling the story one has to select the facts and probabilities which, taken together, constitute the situation confronting the agent. If the story is well told, nothing that is relevant to the decision is left out and not much that is irrelevant to the decision is included in the story; there should be no further questions to be asked about the circumstances before a decision about the right course of action is made, or before a past decision is judged to be right or wrong. Gradually, and by accumulation of examples drawn from experience, belief that the features of the particular case, indefinite in number, are not easily divided into the morally relevant and morally irrelevant will be underlined by the mere process of story-telling.

One cannot establish conclusively by argument in general terms the general conclusion that the morally relevant features of situations encountered cannot be circumscribed. One cannot prove by a prior argument that one does not actually employ a definite criterion of right conduct, specifying a closed set of morally relevant features. One can only appeal to actual examples and call the mind back to personal experience, which will probably include occasions when the particular circumstances of the case modified what would have been the expected and principled decisions, and for reasons which do not themselves enter into any recognized principle.

When lecturing on moral philosophy, I used often to tell a true story of a wartime experience to illustrate moral conflict and to suggest to others that such conflicts are a common experience, and also that they constitute the essence of moral problems, as they are known in most public roles. The episode involved the interrogation of a captured spy, and my difficulty in deciding how he should be treated. The theoretical interest in the story-telling was always in the selection of the circumstances surrounding the interrogation which ought to be included in the story if the complexity of the original moral problem was to be fully reproduced. I noticed that on different occasions, and without any clear intention, I tended to stress different features in the situation as relevant to the problem, and that I did not always even include the same elements of the situation as belonging to the story. Even to speak of 'elements of the situation' and 'features' as included in the story is to oversimplify by a false individuation. I described the episode in different words on different occasions, always under the necessity of omitting some of the circumstances which another person might reasonably consider relevant to the decision. There are always dangers in circumscribing a lived-through situation and in converting it into a definite and clearly stated problem. So often one thinks or says, from the standpoint of the agent: 'So much that mattered has been left out of the story; it was not quite as simple as that'.

The point about false individuation, stressed in *Thought and Action*, is fundamental in the argument against abstraction. Just as we may mislead ourselves by representing situations confronting us as constituted by a definite and final set of elements, so we may also mislead ourselves by representing a tract of our behaviour as constituted by a definite set of distinct actions; how the behaviour over a period of time is broken up into distinct actions is often not unproblematical, even apart from the familiar fact that the same action usually admits of many different descriptions, and that the differences are often relevant to moral judgement. An abstract morality places a prepared grid upon conduct and upon a person's activities and interests, and thereafter one only tends to see the pieces of his conduct and life as they are divided by lines on the grid. From the standpoint of morality, a sceptical nominalism is an aid to thinking.

6

There is another, altogether different reason for rejecting any rational morality, and moral theory, which could be described as 'abstract and computational'. This is the claim that it is of the essence of moral problems that on occasion they seem hopeless, incapable of solution, leaving no right action open; this has been an objection not only to utilitarianism of any form, but to any exactly prescribed moral ideal.

We ordinarily encounter serious moral problems as conflicts between moral claims which, considered *a priori*, seem absolute and exceptionless and which are in fact irreconcilable in the situations that present the problem. Unless one has decided in advance that only one feature of situations is ever of moral concern (for instance, happiness), such situations of conflict between absolute moral claims will occasionally occur and are not to be avoided. Moral theories may be invoked to disguise and to gloss over the conflicts by a variety of strategies: for instance, by denying that the conflicting claims are really absolute claims, or by denying that there is in the long run, and taking a life as a whole, an ultimate conflict. One ideal of rationality requires that behind the apparent conflicts there should be an overall coherence between moral claims and between the most sought after and praised dispositions; they are the necessary constituents of the one supremely desirable way of life.

'Absolute' in 'absolute moral claims' needs explanation. A moral claim, which may be a duty or a right or an obligation, is absolute when it is not conditional upon, or subordinate to, any further moral claim or purpose. A course of action is absolutely forbidden, or absolutely enjoined, if the prohibition or requirement is not conditional upon the presence of any features not mentioned in the prohibition or injunction. The prohibition or injunction contains its own sense, and explains itself. That justice should be done, and should be seen to be done, in a criminal trial is an absolute requirement within the moral convictions of many people, though not of all people: that is, many people believe that, if there is a trial, justice is absolutely required, and this is required irrespective of the circumstances surrounding the trial and irrespective of consequences. Other persons, for example, most utilitarians, would argue that the requirement is a conditional one, and not absolute; good consequences are essential and the requirement would lapse in view of the disastrous consequences of justice in a particular case. That torture of prisoners of any kind under any circumstances is morally wrong is an absolute prohibition within the moral principles of many people. But some would regard it as a conditional prohibition; they might say that in fact there are probably no circumstances in which, all things considered and allowing for the effect of example, torture of prisoners does not in the long run add to the sum of suffering and is permissible. But they would argue that, if there were such circumstances, then the requirement would lapse, because the wrongness comes solely from the suffering.

Two features of moral claims need to be distinguished: (a) a moral claim may be absolute in the sense indicated, namely, that there are no circumstances in which it lapses and ceases to be a moral requirement; (b) a moral claim may be absolute, and yet may come into conflict with another absolute moral claim, with the consequence that one of them is in the final decision overridden, even though it has not lapsed. That a man must not be declared guilty on a criminal charge and punished unless he has been offered legal aid, and unless due process has been observed, may be considered an absolute prohibition, though it is conditional in form. It would not be an absolute prohibition if there were circumstances, not mentioned in the prohibition itself, in which the prohibition would lapse and cease to exist: for example, if the prohibition ceased to exist as soon as the suffering directly caused by observing it clearly exceeded the bad effects of undermining this just rule.

I have argued in chapter 4 that we naturally think, when uncorrupted by theory, of a multiplicity of moral claims, which sometimes come into conflict with each other, just as we think of a multiplicity of human virtues, which sometimes come into conflict with each other; so much so, that if one hears that someone has a moral problem, one immediately assumes that he is confronted with just such a difficult conflict of claims. It is typical and essential, not marginal and accidental, that moral reasoning should be concerned with such conflicts. Unavoidable conflict of principles of conduct, and not a harmony of purposes, is the stuff of morality as we ordinarily experience it, and unless we resolve after reflection to impose a harmony by allowing only one overriding principle of conduct.

'Overriding', like 'absolute', is a word that requires explanation if there is to be an intelligible distinction between a moral claim that lapses, and ceases to exist, under certain conditions and a moral claim that is overridden. One may have a moral obligation to assist one's partner in a joint enterprise when he calls on one in difficulties; but this obligation may lapse, or cease to exist, if he later makes it clear that he no longer wishes to incur such an obligation on his side. This situation of lapse is to be contrasted with a situation in which your obligation to assist your partner is in unexpected circumstances overriden by urgent considerations of public policy, which imposes duties of overriding importance on you, duties that cannot be fulfilled if your obligation is to be fulfilled. There is a conflict, and one is pulled in two different directions by moral claims that remain in force. The obligation does not lapse, or cease to exist; nothing has happened which removes its basis and nullifies or cancels it. Equally, in the familiar case of a conflict of absolute duties, for instance, a conflict between the duty to be impartial and just in adjudications and the duty to help the distressed and oppressed; both duties remain and neither is destroyed by coming into conflict with the other.

We are prompted to theorize about morality partly because such conflicts notoriously arise. If a harmony of principles and dispositions seemed attainable, the problem of giving a rational reconstruction of acceptable moral judgements, and of their grounds, would seem directly soluble. But we know from direct experience that it is our nature to be pulled in contrary directions by the principles that are acceptable to us and in respect of the dispositions that we admire and that we wish to have.

The point could be put in another way. If our moral intuitions seemed to form a harmonious system of compatible claims, there would be a less radical difference between animals guided by instinct, in accordance with natural laws, towards their natural way of life and human beings guided by moral intuitions, which would also guide them towards the one way of life that has to be presumed to be natural to them. But we in fact find that a conflict of moral claims is natural to us, and that there are contrary dispositions that are immediately admirable and desirable. We not only find these conflicts in our unreflective intuitions and in commonplace morality; we may also find, after reflection on the source and nature of our moral intuitions, that these conflicts are unavoidable and not to be softened or glossed over. It seems an unavoidable feature of moral experience that men should be torn between the moral claims entailed by effectiveness in action, and particularly in politics, and the moral claims derived from the ideals of scrupulous honesty and integrity: between candour and kindness: between spontaneity and conscientious care: between open-mindedness, seeing both sides of a case, and loyalty to a cause. Such dispositions as these, and the contrary moral claims associated with them, generate the more difficult moral problems, because morality originally appears in our experience as a conflict of claims and a division of purpose.

An ideal of rationality is the instrument sometimes used to soften and to eliminate such conflicts as these; and this result is achieved by showing that the reasons that explain apparently conflicting moral claims form a coherent system and lead back to a common basis, to a single reason behind all moral claims. This was the argument of Plato's *Republic*, and the same theme is pursued by moral philosophers who are consequentialists, explaining away contrary moral claims as uncertainty about outcomes.

What is the force, and what is the consequence, of denying any ideal of rationality for practical reason that entails the softening or elimination of ultimate conflicts? Is there an *a priori* and general argument which corresponds to the argument from rationality and which shows that ineliminable conflicts among moral claims are to be expected by wise and truthful men, and not an ultimate harmony among moral claims? It is part of the force of the denial of harmony that no sufficient reason of any kind is on occasion available to explain a decision made after careful reflection in a situation of moral conflict; and that this lack of sufficient reason is not ground for apology, because our divided, and comparatively open, nature requires one to choose, without sufficient reason, between irreconcilable dispositions and contrary claims; there is unavoidably a breakdown of clear reasoning in choosing what the future is to be, because the reflective and second-order desires which, coupled with beliefs, guide the choices point to goals which are irreconcilable in the actual world and are harmonised only in an ideal world. That there should be a conflict between reflective desires, unreconciled outside an ideal world, is itself a condition of continuing moral development, both of the individual and of the species. In the history of an individual the choices that he makes in conflicts between duties and reflective inclinations and purposes will constitute his own character as an individual. The causes explaining his choice will not all be found in rational assent to a theory. His imagination of possibilities has its part, and so do intuitions that he cannot fully explain, arising from experience.

7

Sometimes, and particularly often in politics and government, the decision in a situation of conflict involves a trade-off; for instance, a certain amount of liberty for the individual is traded off in exchange for a clear general increase in welfare. Sufficient reason is on some occasions lacking in such decisions because there is still no compelling principle, or rational method, of balancing one value against another. But there is a more radical lack of sufficient reason in cases where it would be misleading to speak of a trade-off; this is where a conflict between different ways of life arises and where there is no way of achieving a reasonable and coherent compromise between them. The conflict is not between two values which in more fortunate circumstances could both be realized; but it is a conflict between two ways of life neither of which could ever be fully realized without some deliberate impairment of the other. Perhaps one could never in politics be entirely loyal and helpful to one's personal friends and entirely impartial and effective in serving the public interest; sooner or later there will in the common course of things be a conflict, as loyalty entails partiality. One could properly speak of a trade-off if one were trying to combine a decent degree of loyalty to friends with a decent degree of impartiality. The trade-off between antithetical values would then be the pursuit of an Aristotelian balance, an intuitive moral compromise that repudiates two extremes on either side. The Aristotelian balance between public and private life, with their attached virtues, and between practical and theoretical interests, is a feature of that particular way of life. The pressing moral problems within this way of life are problems of priorities, which can equally well be thought of as trade-offs; how do I balance the moral claims of friendship against the duties of public life? In a complete life a defensible order of priorities can be with luck achieved and with luck an overall balance realized; and this is the moral ideal within this way of life, the Aristotelian ideal.

There is a well-known and radical type of conflict in which there is no trade-off and no compromise and no striking of a balance. He has a yes or no choice, which can be represented as a choice between two moral claims, one of which will be taken to override the other; a choice also between two characters that may in future be imputed to him, as a person dedicated to his particular mission or as a person cherishing his family; a choice between two ways of life, both of which are presented by moral claims which he acknowledges. He may invoke a number of religious or philosophical or historical beliefs in support of his choice; 'ultimate' does not mean the same as 'unargued' and 'unsupported'. But he has no recourse to already established beliefs of his which are also moral beliefs. The whole framework of moral belief has been called in question by this particular conflict.

Any actual choice between two ways of life, which comes to a head in a particular conflict of duties, arises from dense personal experience, and as a consequence of someone's particular conditions of life, and of his philosophical beliefs. No more can be said in general terms, except that morality does unalterably have this aspect of commitment to a way of life, even though many persons may never consciously confront such an ultimate choice. They are ready to recognize the possibility of an ultimate conflict. They are aware of an openness at the margin of morality and in their own way of life. There is some wilfulness, as well as naturalness, in the structure of practice and belief that they have accepted or imposed, and they recognize this, when they reflect. They know that they may be confronted with a conflict of duties which expresses a point of divergence between two ways of life, both of which have a nobility and worth, but which cannot under actual conditions be combined. A decision in an ultimate conflict may commit the agent to a way of life, which will extend in time indefinitely, as far as he knows, and, as far as he knows, it will close certain possibilities to him for ever, even though they are possibilities that he had thought of as being very highly desirable and valuable.

In private life, and outside politics, a one-sided commitment, the incurring of a very great cost in valuable activity renounced, sometimes seems an overriding requirement, just as sometimes the striking of a balance between conflicting claims sometimes seems an overriding moral requirement. There is no superior principle that is invoked in deciding between these two possibilities. To some people a narrow specialization of achievement presents itself as an overriding moral requirement because of some outstanding value, perhaps of aesthetics or of science or religion, to which they are committed to the exclusion of all others; to others the neglect of competing moral claims, which the specialisation entails, is repugnant and seems inhuman, and they reject it as impossible from a moral point of view. That there should be both these irreconcilable opinions, and that one mind might not unreasonably oscillate between them, is expected in the common order of experience, and is familiar from episodes in history and in literature. Every reflective person has had the experience of oscillating between two possible descriptions of his own conduct, whether it is actual conduct or only envisaged conduct; one correct description makes the conduct acceptable and not to be despised, and the other correct description mentions features of the conduct which make it morally questionable and regrettable. Two competing ways of life, between which a person chooses, explicitly or implicitly, may impose different descriptions on the same envisaged conduct, which may emerge as prohibited in virtue of the descriptions relevant to one way of life and as positively required within another way of life. It is not only that the priorities to be aimed at are different in the two ways of life, both in respect of moral claims and of dispositions; but also the questions that one asks about a course of conduct, before evaluating it, will tend to be different.

8

It should now be possible to exhibit the principal differences between public morality and the morality of private life rather more clearly. In both spheres of practical thinking, which obviously overlap, 'abstract computational morality' properly has a pejorative sense, for the reasons given. The model of practical reasoning in difficult and substantial cases oversimplifies the difficulties by over-assimulation to reasoning in theoretical inquiries which demand coherence; it leaves too little place for intuitive discrimination alongside abstract general principles and the explicit computation of consequences. But the differences between public and private life have forced themselves on men's attention, and they enter into Machiavelli's perennial problem of the necessity of 'dirty hands' in great political and social enterprises. The evident elements of Machiavelli's problem can be listed:

(a) Public policy is a greater thing, as Aristotle remarked, and an agent in the public domain normally has responsibility for greater and more enduring consequences and for consequences that change more men's lives.
(b) Violence, and the threat of violence or of force, have always been in prospect in public life and in the execution of public policies. In the normal run of things the moral problems associated with the use of force, and with war and violence, do not now arise in private life. The occasional use of violence, and the normal uses of force and of threats of force, introduce their own moral conflicts.
(c) In modern politics, and particularly in a democracy, one is reasonably required to protect the interests of those whom one in some sense represents, whether they be one's followers in a party or fellow citizens. There are obligations and duties specifically attached to representative roles.

Taking (a) and (c) together, the conclusion to be drawn is that there is an added responsibility in public affairs, and, secondly, this responsibility falls more heavily on the consequences of policies in the lives and fortunes of great numbers of persons unknown to those forming the policies.

Machiavelli stressed this conclusion more vividly than any other writer ever has. He argued that it was irresponsible and morally wrong to apply to political action the moral standards that are appropriate to private life and to personal relations: standards of friendship and of justice. If one refused to be ruthless in pursuit of objectives in public policy, and refused to use deceit and guile as instruments of policy, one betrayed those who had put their trust in the person who represents them. Deceit and violence and the breaking of promises and undertakings are normal in the relations between states, and it seemed unlikely, in the sixteenth century, that they would cease to be normal. Public policies are rightly judged by their consequences, not by the intrinsic quality of the acts involved in their execution, which, when considered separately, are often unacceptable in the light of the moral standards of private life. Machiavelli implied that morality in politics must be a consequentialist morality, and the 'must' here marks a moral injunction. A fastidiousness about the means employed, appropriate in personal relations, is a moral dereliction in a politician, and the relevant moral criterion for a great national enterprise is lasting success; and success is measured by a historian's yardstick: continuing power, prosperity, high national spirit, a long-lasting dominance of the particular state or nation in the affairs of men: so Machiavelli argued. Below the level of state politics, any representative role or official position, which confers power, to some degree imposes a responsibility for the well-being of persons not directly known.

There is a further ground of distinction between public and private morality: that there is a greater requirement of explicitness of reasoning in public morality than in private. Partly because of the bias towards a consequentialist criterion, and partly because of representative roles in politics, there is a requirement that an agent in politics should be able to give an account of the reasons for his policies. He normally needs an endorsement that his policies are right from his followers; and he needs to be understood by his followers, who will otherwise tend to distrust him if they do not know, or do not think that they know, how he thinks about substantial moral issues and what his calculations of consequences are. In summary, there is a requirement that his actions should fit together into explicitly formulated policies with more or less clearly specified consequences in view. When a policy is attacked, appeals to intuitions of right and wrong will usually not be an adequate defence. In private life such appeals often have a natural place in answering criticism, because it is recognized that the judgement required is not principally a judgement of calculable consequences, but of more complex and disparate values; and also of some values which do not involve calculation of consequences, in matters of love and friendship and fairness and integrity.

The moral infamies of the American intervention in Vietnam are not to be imputed to the fact that American policy-makers looked to the future, calculating consequences in resisting communist expansion, but to the fact that their calculations were not tempered by respect for the ordinary moral decencies. The fault was not in the fact of calculation, but in the extreme crudity, the insensitiveness and lack of perception, the false definiteness and false clarity of the calculations. An illusory image of rationality distorted the moral judgement of the American policy-makers. They thought that their opponents in the USA were sentimental and guided only by their unreflective emotions, while they, the policy-makers, were computing consequences with precision and objectivity, using quasi-quantitative methods. They had the minimum of natural feeling for, and perception of, the peculiar mechanical brutality and unfeelingness of their conduct of the war, as it appeared to those who were not calculating so simply. The necessary blend between rational policy-making on the one side and natural feelings and reflective intuitions of right and wrong on the other had been distorted by a naive and mechanical Machiavellianism, which finally failed. The policy-makers were corrupted in judgement of consequences by the pseudo-rationalistic vocabulary in which they discussed 'options'. Under the influence of bad social science, and the bad moral philosophy that usually goes with it, they oversimplified the moral issues and provided an example of false rationality.

9

The public policies of any interest group or party normally have a theoretical background in a commonly professed set of moral beliefs. Specific policies need to be referred back to the set of moral beliefs which are held in common within the social or national group or party. A moral conflict, which expresses a division between two ways of life, is often a division of loyalties, and often entails more than an isolated individual choice; it often entails a political commitment.

I am not arguing that different moralities, in the sense of different sets of prescriptions, are to be applied in private and in public life, as if these were self-contained spheres of activity. The claim is rather that the assumption of a political role, and of powers to change men's lives on a large scale, carry with them not only new responsibilities, but a new kind of responsibility, which entails, first, accountability to one's followers; secondly, policies that are to be justified principally by their eventual consequences; and, thirdly, a withholding of some of the scruples that in private life would prohibit one from using people as a means to an end and also from using force and deceit. The differences in these respects are matters of degree and of balance, but they are real differences. In addition to moral seriousness in justice and fairness to individuals, in love and friendship, constituting the sphere of private life, there is also political seriousness, seriousness in the use of power; and this requires higher priority for some duties and corresponding virtues and lower priority for refinements. In particular, it requires priority for duties of careful and responsible calculation, for the virtues of prudence and 'cleverness', cleverness being that Aristotelian component in moral virtue which political responsibility demands.

10

The three-tiered conception of morality outlined in chapter 4 is designed to make intelligible the complex relation of private and political morality. Conflict between competing ways of life – religious, ideological, national, family and class conflict – has been perpetual, and conflict is always to be expected; and the conflicts are not only in the realm of ideas, but are often also political conflicts, involving force and the threat of force. A way of life is protected and maintained by the exercise of political power, and that way of life will evolve, and will change with changing forms of knowledge, as long as sufficient political protection of it lasts.

But one must not exaggerate the historical, time-dependent elements in admired and desired and sought after ways of life. There are evident uniformities in the virtues of love and friendship and justice, and in the more pressing moral claims recognized in almost any known social organization above the most primitive level. There is some constancy in the virtues almost universally recognized as essential in any person who is to be praised and respected as a person. The difference comes in the priorities among the virtues recognized in different ways of life, subject to different historical circumstances, and in the duties, rights and obligations consequently recognized, and in the priorities among these various moral claims.

11

Moral theory cannot be rounded off and made complete and tidy; partly because so much that is of value in a human life depends upon uncontroll-able accident, partly because we still know so little about the determinants of behaviour and about human nature generally, partly because indi-viduals vary so greatly in their dispositions and interests, partly because new ways of life should always be expected to arise in association with new knowledge and with new social forms. There is one further reason; we expect also leaps of the imagination, moments of insight, very rarely, and in unusual men, which will lead to transformations of experience and to new moral ambitions and to new enjoyments of living.

6

Morality and Convention

1

The philosophical dispute about the objectivity of morals has been four, or more, disputes rolled into one. First, there is the argument about predicates standing for moral qualities; are they to be construed as intrinsic qualities of actions or situations? Secondly, there is the rather different dispute as to whether to attribute a moral quality to a person or to an action is properly to be taken as describing that person or action, or to be taken as another kind of performance, for example, as expressing an attitude, or as recommending conduct, or both. Thirdly, there is the question of whether two persons expressing disagreement about the answer to a moral problem are properly described as contradicting each other, which is usually interpreted as a question about the conditions of applicability of 'true' and 'false' to moral judgements. Fourthly, there is the related, but different, question of whether there is a respectable procedure, recognized in other contexts, for establishing the acceptability of moral judgements of various kinds, or whether moral judgement is in this respect *sui generis* and for this reason problematic.

These four are some, certainly not all, of the clearly distinguishable questions that are to be found in the literature.

2

There is another essential issue, which was best expressed in the ancient controversy about whether moral discriminations are to be accepted as true or correct, when they are true, in virtue of custom, convention and law (*νόμῳ*) or whether they are true in virtue of the nature of things (*φύσει*). By an essential issue I here mean an issue which unavoidably arises for thinking men, independently of any theories in philosophy, when they reflect on the apparent stringency and unavoidability of their more disagreeable duties and obligations, and when they ask themselves where this apparent unavoidability comes from. That there is a clear and unavoidable distinction between moral judgements or beliefs issuing from reason and judgements issuing from sentiment is not evident to someone who has not heard of, or is not convinced by, the philosophies of mind that are built around these psychological terms. No philosophical theories have to be invoked when a man encounters, in experience or in reading, the actual variety of moral beliefs and practices, and the overlapping similarities between different moral systems, and then asks himself how these differences and similarities are to be interpreted. Do they represent the kind of differences, and the kind of similarities, that one finds, for instance, in different conventions in dress, in personal ornament, in ideals of feminine elegance, in social manners while eating, in dietary conventions? Or do they represent the kinds of difference and similarity that are found in ideals or norms of physical health and of good food? We are disposed at first sight to think of differences and similarities between the discriminations in the first list as differences and similarities in conventions. We are apt to think of the differences and similarities in the second list – ideals or norms of health and of food – as differences and similarities in the assessment of independently testable and objective norms and therefore as differences in nature. We are apt to think that any variety of judgements about good health, which there may be, is simply evidence that there are a number of false or inaccurate opinions on this subject, because there is a standard of good health which medical science can expound and which rests on clearly demonstrable differences in natural processes: similarly for good food, in the sense of food that nourishes.

These two contrasting lists, and the explanation of the contrast, clearly represent only a first, unanalysed and naive view of the Greek distinction between nature and convention. But it is at least clear that there is an accepted contrast between those norms or ideals which are expected to be highly diverse, and which are not expected, and which are not required, to converge on the one hand, and those norms or ideals which (a) refer to ascertainable natural facts, and (b) are more or less constant responses to more or less constant human needs and interests, and therefore (c) where there is a well-established expectation of convergence.

A clear example of a norm or ideal which is essentially diverse and non-converging is to be found in the arrangement of hair in either sex prevailing at different times and in different cultures. First, there is no requirement that forms of arrangement of hair in men and women should converge towards a single norm or ideal, any more than there is a requirement that norms of elegance in dress or other kinds of adornment should converge. I shall argue that there is even a *prima facie* requirement that they diverge and remain various. But there is a requirement that all rational persons should arrive at a consensus about what constitutes health, if only because health is an ideal which all normal men in all normal conditions and at all normal times want to pursue. Because bad health causes pain and death, it is natural that people in all places at all times should attach at least some considerable value to good health, and that good health should count as a fundamental and constant need and not only as a contingent interest. But there are no ascertainable natural facts which, taken together with more or less constant human needs or interests, imply that one or other arrangement of hair, or manner of adornment, is the most desirable. Partly for this reason both Plato and Aristotle, wishing to stress the objectivity, and the naturalness, of moral distinctions, dwelt on an analogy between the health of the body and the health of the soul; and health of the soul is naturally expressed in moral virtue and just conduct.

But more has to be said about 'nature' and natural in this context: the traditional idea of moral distinctions as founded in the nature of things implies that there is an underlying structure of moral distinctions, partly concealed by the variety of actual moral beliefs, a structure that is defensible by rational argument and by common observation of human desires and sentiments, when a covering of local prejudices and superstitions has been removed. If the underlying structure of moral distinctions has no supernatural source, it must be recognized by rational inquiry as having its origin in nature and, specifically, in human nature: that is, in constant human needs and interests, and in canons of rational calculation. So in Aristotle: so also, in a contemporary continuation, in Rawls's *A Theory of Justice*, which notoriously argues that rational choosers, having taken account of entirely general, non-discriminating facts about human nature, will be led to recognize a certain set of principles, constituting a first framework of just institutions, as being evidently reasonable. The most general non-discriminating facts about normal human needs and interests, with human nature taken as it is, are put together with a model of rationality to derive an idea of the principles of justice. This skeletal idea of justice, therefore, has a claim to acceptance by all rational persons at all times and everywhere, and the claim is independent of the variety of prevailing interests and sentiments which distinguish populations at different times and places from one another: independent, that is, of specific cultural factors. *A fortiori* the rationally preferred idea of justice is independent of the variety of interests and sentiments which distinguish individuals from each other.

Rationality; a claim to universal acceptance; naturalness: these three properties of the idea of justice, as typically presented by Rawls, are connected within a single argument. The argument is designed to uncover a core of shared rationality, which is the natural distinguishing mark of the species as a whole, and which is typically revealed by a stripping-down procedure. The stripping-down removes a supposed overlay, or dressing, of local custom, of distinctive cultural factors, and removes the moral idiosyncrasies of individuals, which have their local explanations and their temporary causes. These local causes, studied by historians and anthropologists, are evidently changeable and transient, as social systems and cultures change and decay. Because the moral prescriptions and claims are to be explained by temporary and local interests, the duties and obligations prescribed exist by convention rather than in the nature of the things. No convergence towards universal agreement is claimed for this set of prescriptions, in contrast with the principles of justice.

Claims of justice have always been the preferred examples of moral claims that are to be recognized by reason, and as founded in the nature of things, as not essentially diverse, and as not contingent upon any specific type of social order. Plato could argue that the foundations of ethics are to be found in the nature of things, not in convention or in the arbitrary will of powerful men, partly by representing justice as the principal virtue of an individual and of a social order, as health is of the body.

3

If one contrasts justice as a human good with love and friendship, one expects to find that justice prescribes a comparatively fixed, and also a comparatively specific, set of norms for human conduct. One will expect to find that love and friendship, always good things and no less to be desired, require specifically different types of behaviour, and different relationships, in different social contexts; superficially and pre-theoretically, the specific realizations of love and friendship seem likely not to conform to a fixed and definite norm as the specific realizations of justice are expected to conform to a fixed and definite norm, and to principles that can be formulated. One does not normally speak of principles of love and friendship, as of principles of justice and fairness.

We have the idea that the specific forms of love and friendship must vary with the different kinship systems and social roles that prevail in different societies, while the principles of justice do not have varying forms, although the circumstances to which they are applied may differ. So we may think that there is at least a difference of degree between moral claims that prescribe just conduct, which purport to be derived from rationally defensible principles, and moral claims that prescribe conduct that counts as friendly or as a manifestation of love; and that this contrast arises within morality.

One may concede that there are just these differences of degree between virtues that have specific and determinate realizations, and that are everywhere and at all times very similar in their behavioural expressions, and virtues that have realizations differing according to the different conventions and social roles in different societies. But perhaps this is only a difference of degree. To take one example, Aristotle's chapters on justice in the Nicomachean Ethics bear about as close a resemblance to a representative modern treatise on justice such as Rawls's, as Aristotle's chapters on love and friendship bear to some later treatise on that subject, for example, that of Montaigne or Stendhal. Perhaps more strange omissions, and strangeness generally, will strike a contemporary ear when reading Aristotle's account of the moral significance of love and friendship, and the strangeness of tone and detail may be rather less when a contemporary reader considers Aristotle on justice. On the other hand Aristotle notoriously does not see a contravention of principles of justice in slavery, and was generally much less inclined than modern theorists to count unequal distributions of primary goods as generally unfair.

To notice a disputable difference of degree among and within the recognized virtues in this respect still leaves the more fundamental question: taking different moralities as wholes, are they not all *partly* human artifices, and to be defended partly by appeals to the imagination, rather than to reason, in the sense in which social manners are partly a human artifice, and to be defended partly by appeals to the imagination, and in the sense in which works of literature and sculpture and drama are wholly human artifices, and to be assessed by the imagination?

Within this notion of artificiality and artifice a distinction has to be made. Let it be agreed that there are some definite and comparatively clear restraints, argumentatively and rationally defensible, upon what conduct, and what social arrangements, can at any time and anywhere be counted as just and fair. With justice the notion of imagination seems out of place, and reason, and reasonable considerations, are alone in place, as in the establishment of rules of law. The setting in which just conduct and just and fair arrangements are distinguished from unjust ones is an argumentative setting, a judicial setting with a verdict in view, and with a contest between rational considerations always a possibility. In so far as artificiality is taken to imply, or is associated with, the imagination and with imaginative invention, the principles of justice must be represented as not artificial, just because they are intended to be principles solely defensible by rational argument. In this respect justice is to be contrasted with love and friendship because the prescriptions that express these virtues may be justified, as manifestations of love and friendship, by appeals to imagination as much as to reason. New forms and varieties of love and friendship are brought into existence and are recognized as new forms, and are recognized even as new kinds of love and friendship. This recognition is not defensible by rational considerations without any appeals to imagination; one has to envisage a particular person or persons in a particular situation and to invent or to recognize a form of behaviour that seems to be right in the peculiar circumstances. There is not the same requirement of convergence just because reasonable argument is less in place in such cases of envisaging the right conduct in the particular circumstances. There is no obvious requirement that everyone at all times should love and be friendly in the same way, or in accordance with fixed principles that can be formulated and defended.

The contrast in respect of artificiality between the rational virtue of justice and the not entirely rational virtue of love or friendship might be explained by distinguishing two kinds of artificiality. The transition from a state of nature, in which men act according to their unmoralized and unsocialized impulses, is usually represented as a rationally intelligible improvement of life chances for all men, wherever they are and at all times. They conclude a contract among themselves, and their descendants, making the same calculation all over again as reasonable men, are ready always to ratify this contract. There is a sense in which the reasonably just social arrangements, and the structure of law and of the constitution, which emerge from the supposed original contract, are artificial; certainly they are constructions of human reason to restrict and control natural forces. But there is the other sense in which just arrangements, being largely independent of culturally modified preferences and interests, are natural to all human beings, who are as a species capable of a true appreciation of their own permanent nature, using their reason.

4

In the Greek argument, we are told to contrast the great variety of social customs prevailing in different places and at different times with those fundamental principles of desirable or acceptable human associations which emerge from the ideal social contract. No rational reconstruction or transcendental deduction of these divergent social customs is to be attempted. In Herodotus and Xenophon you are led to expect that social customs will diverge, and that different populations will distinguish themselves, and identify themselves, both in their own minds and in the minds of others, by their customs. Part of the point of the customs resides in their diversity, in the discriminations that they mark. The glory of being Greek emerged in following the social customs, the habits in matters of address and social manners and in conduct generally, which are distinctively Greek; and the glory of being Athenian, or being Spartan, rather than of being just any Greek, resided in following the very different and distinctive customs of these two very discriminating cities. If the word 'glory' seems too high flown and seems an exaggeration in this context, one could say instead that the point of thinking of oneself as Greek or as Athenian resided in the thought of the distinctiveness of their way of life; and their way of life consisted not only of social customs and habits of address and habits of conduct more generally, but also of distinctive moral codes and principles, with typical prescriptions derived from them. This implies that no convergence to general agreement is required in a justification of these prescriptions.

When one values the customs and morality of one's own society or group as distinctive, one is thinking of them as discriminatory. So far there is no requirement to universalize the prescriptions, implicit or explicit, which govern the customs and values, and to think of the prescriptions as applicable to all men, whatever their condition. Equally the converse is not entailed either; that the customs and peculiar moral prescriptions of a particular group ought to be confined to that group. One could consistently think of one's own moral virtues and dispositions as at present existing only among one's own people, say, the Greeks, and at the same time consistently believe that the barbarians ought to adopt Greek moral prescriptions and dispositions and ought to cease to be barbarians. If one looks at the customs from another angle, it does not even follow from the fact that one takes pride in the thought that one's own habits and dispositions are distinctive and different, and that they constitute a definite identity for the group to which one belongs, that one thinks that all men should belong to groups which have distinctive habits and dispositions. None of these strong conclusions is entailed. The recognition of distinctiveness, and the moral endorsement of it, only entail that there are acceptable moral prescriptions which are not to be defended and justified by the kind of rational argument, which enters into ideal social contract theory, whether in Plato, Hobbes, Locke, Rousseau or Rawls. The prescriptions have to be defended and justified in a quite different way.

5

In what way? How do these non-convergent moral claims and prescriptions differ in the defence and justification offered for them from those that can be defended and justified by a rational argument, as the principles of justice can be, by the stripping down argument, that is, by the argument that a common requirement of justice, and of the broad principles of justice, would be recognized by all rational men who abstract from their contingent and divergent interests?

In order to distinguish moral prescriptions from mere custom and social manners, first one should distinguish between dispositions and habits, and accompanying prescriptions, which are taken very seriously and to which importance is attached, and those which are regarded as comparatively trivial and unimportant; and the test is the kind and degree of the feeling of shock and repugnance and disapproval which would normally occur when the custom or habit is not followed; and, secondly, whether this feeling is a reflective one, and survives after it is evaluated, or whether it is merely an immediate reaction to be explained away by personal factors. The strong repugnance and disapproval, which after reflection seems to the subject appropriate to the particular case, would normally be accounted a moral attitude and a moral emotion, resting on a moral judgement of the case; the subject would think of his repugnance and his disapproval as a moral attitude implying a moral judgement: not just a matter of custom and social propriety. His reflection on his attitude, and on the implied judgement, would be an attempt to detach himself from reactions which he thought could not be defended and justified on a clear and calm consideration of the case, but could only be explained by features of his own temperament.

To claim impartiality in judgement, in this sense, is not to claim that the judgement is one that rational persons must assent to if they are similarly impartial, which is the claim made for judgements about fundamental principles of justice. A reflective repugnance and moral disapproval, and implied moral judgement, may be concentrated upon a breach of a moral code, say a code of honour, which is an essential element in the way of life of a particular social group, a group that takes pride in this distinction, in the way in which a Welsh nationalist or a Basque nationalist may take pride in speaking and preserving their particular languages, which are also essential elements in their ways of life. They may consistently admit that people of different origins and having different roles may rightly, or at least reasonably, follow quite different and incompatible rules. So far from wishing to generalize the distinctive moral claims to which he is reflectively committed, a person proud of his culture may contrast these moral claims, in virtue of their distinctiveness, with the moral claims of justice and reasonable benevolence, or of concern for happiness, which he specifically counts as universal claims, arising from a shared humanity and an entirely general norm of reasonableness. He may agree that he can easily conceive of alternative rules which are neither more nor less reasonable; for reasonableness is not the prime consideration in this sphere. He will not be disturbed by evidence that in other societies quite different rules or conventions prevail among entirely reasonable persons, who would broadly agree with him about the principles of justice and about a necessary concern with happiness.

There are good reasons to expect that most people have been, and always will be, ready to acknowledge both kinds of moral claim, the universal and convergent moral claim, and the distinctive moral claim, which is to be defended by direct reference to one actually existing way of life in which it is a necessary element, and to the imagination of particular cases which arise within this way of life. The good reasons for distinguishing the two are repeatedly foreshadowed in the literature of moral and political philosophy: for example, in Hegel's criticisms of the abstractness of Kant's rational will and moral law, and in Burke's criticisms of the morality of the French Enlightenment. As morality cannot be separated from canons of practical reasoning and of prudence, and from the rational foundations of law and justice on the one side, so it cannot be separated from social manners and customs, and habits of thought and speech, and the distinctive elements of a culture on the other side – at least under known normal conditions, and until humanity is transformed, as both utilitarians and Kantians have wished that it should be, though for quite different reasons. Personal relations between people within families and kinship systems, and in love and friendship; sexual customs and prohibitions; duties and obligations associated with the dead and with ancestors and with death itself; rituals and customs that express social solidarity in different kinds of institution; customs and prohibitions in war: it is a genuinely universal requirement of morality that there should be some rules or customs governing conduct in these areas of strong emotions. The rules and customs observed in these areas, particularly those of sexuality and the family, constitute much of the central core of a way of life, even though they are subject to general principles of social justice and of benevolence. I may for many reasons want my actual way of life, inherited and developed, to be modified or changed; but it is still the starting-point of my morality, the bedrock of my moral dispositions, upon which I must build differently.

More than a pride in distinctiveness and a more definite sense of identity is involved in the acknowledgement of moral claims in the areas mentioned, claims that are not to be adequately defended by a rational calculation of common human necessities. Just as any natural language has to satisfy the common requirements of language as such, being a means of communication, so on the other side a language has to develop in history, and over a period of time, its own distinguishing forms and vocabulary, if it is to have any hold on men's imagination and memory. The project of Esperanto, the generally shared and syncretistic language, does not succeed. A language distinguishes a particular people with a particular shared history and with a particular set of shared associations and with largely unconscious memories, preserved in the metaphors that are imbedded in the vocabulary. So also with some parts of morality: for example, the prohibitions and prescriptions that govern sexual morality and family relationships and the duties of friendship.

6

Reasons can be given for these two faces of morality: the law-like and rational, the language-like and imaginative: that men are not only rational and calculative in forming and pursuing their ideals and in maintaining rules of conduct, but they are also in the grip of particular and distinguishing memories and of particular and distinguishing local passions; and the Aristotelian word to emphasize is 'particular'. Love and affection are necessarily concentrated on a particular person or a particular place, as a disposition to justice is directed towards a general rule or a repeatable process. A disposition to love and to friendship is a central virtue, and it has always been recognized as such, no less than justice and courage. Justice is the disposition to treat all men and women alike in certain respects, in recognition of their common humanity: love and friendship are dispositions to treat men and women very differently, in recognition of their individuality and unrepeated nature. The species is sustained and prolonged by sexual drives and by family ties which are necessarily to some degree exclusive and particularized. It is precisely the basic biological phenomena of sex and family relationships, of childhood, youth and age which, being obviously natural, are modified by diverse and distinctive conventions and filtered through various restraints, some morally trivial and some not. Any particular sexual morality is under-determined by purely rational considerations, which are everywhere valid. Defence and justification will also take the form of pointing to the distinctive and peculiar virtues of one way of life, to its history and to the reciprocal dependence of the elements of this way of life on each other. At all times and in all places there has to be a sexual morality which is recognized; but it does not have to be the same sexual morality with the same restraints and prescription. The rational requirement is the negative one: that the rules and conventions should not cause evident and avoidable unhappiness or offend accepted principles of fairness. These bare requirements plainly under-determine the full, complex morality of the family and of sexual relationships and of friendship in any person's actual way of life. One particular sexual morality is an integral and indispensable part of a way of life which actually exists, one among others, and which the judging subject believes ought to be preserved as a valuable way of life, actually realized, not perfect, but still valuable. But rational argument is not available below the level of the general requirements of fairness and of utility; and the lower level of specific habits and specific conventions is of binding importance in sexual morality.

The kind of 'must not' that arises within this area of morality can be compared with a linguistic prohibition, for example, that you must not split an infinitive: a particular rule of a particular language, which is not made less binding by the fact that it is not a general rule in language. The grammar and rules of propriety in any particular language may seem arbitrary and artificial when compared with the general logical framework of language, or with some presumed deep structure in all languages. The grammar is arbitrary and in this sense artificial only to the degree that it is not to be explained by the natural needs of communication and of thought alone, but must also be explained supplementarily by reference to a particular history of the language's development; and even this supplementary explanation will almost certainly be incomplete and will fall short because of the complexity of the relationships involved. Alongside languages and in social customs, everyone recognizes that there must be rules and conventions of conduct that deserve to be called moral in certain definite areas; and everyone also recognizes that these rules (a) must fit into, and be compatible with, universal, rationally explicable principles of justice and utility analogous to a deep structure in language; and (b) that the strict rules within these limits will be diverse and will seem arbitrary, because they have historically performed the function of distinguishing one social group from all others.

How then does one balance the partly conventional moral claims against rationally defensible principles of justice and of utility, the claims of pure rational morality? The condensed and cryptic answer that men are only half-rational carries the implication that our desires and purposes are always permeated by memories and by local attachments and by historical associations, just as they are always permeated by rational calculation; and that this will always be true. There is a rational justification for respecting some set of not unreasonable moral claims of a conventional kind, because some moral prescriptions are necessary in the areas of sexuality and family relationships and friendship and social customs and attitudes to death; and that men are reasonably inclined to respect those prescriptions which have in fact survived and which have a history of respect, unless they find reasons to reject them drawn from moral considerations of the opposing rational type. It evidently does not follow from the fact that a way of life has survived, and that it has some hold over men's sentiments and loyalties, that that way of life, with the moral claims which are a necessary element of it, ought for these reasons to be protected and prolonged: there may well be overriding reasons of a rational kind against these claims – that they are unfair or that they destroy happiness.

7

The degree of permeation by local memories and local attachments varies with different human interests: at its greatest where emotions and passions have an instinctual foundation, as in sexual and family relationships, and less extensive in areas where rational calculation guides passions, as in the morality surrounding property relations and ownership.

Exactly in those areas of experience where natural impulses and emotions are strongest, and where rational control and direction are weak, distinctive and conventional moral prohibitions are naturally in place and naturally respected: and they are respected for reasons largely independent of justice and of the avoidance of harm and the promotion of welfare. To take a familiar example, the proper treatment of the dead, whatever the obligatory treatment may be in any particular society, has always been at the centre of moralities, and failure to bury the dead, or to do whatever is locally accounted necessary, has always been morally shocking. The force of particular moral claims of this type is not to be explained by general principles of justice or of benevolence and welfare. That the dead must be appropriately disposed of, even at a high cost, is a very general requirement, and a mark of humanity; but it is also generally recognized that what is appropriate for one people, and one set of circumstances, is not generally appropriate elsewhere. The fact that there is no general requirement of convergence is not an indication that the moral duty of respect for the dead, and the appropriate custom, is not to be taken seriously. Freud's superb essay 'On Mourning' helps to explain the complementary relation between nature and convention here.

We are unavoidably born into both a natural order and a cultural order, and old age, death, family and friendship are among the natural phenomena which have to be moralized by conventions and customs, within one culture or other, and that means within a very particular and specific set of moral requirements. The one unnatural, and impossible, cry is the consequentialist's: 'Away with convention: anything goes provided that it does not interfere with welfare or with principles of justice'.

To summarize: to the old question of whether moral claims are *νόμῳ* or *φύσει*, conventional or in the nature of things, like norms of social propriety or like norms of health, 'both' is my answer. There are two kinds of moral claim – those that, when challenged are referred to universal needs of human beings and to their reasonable calculations, which should be the same everywhere, and hence to the stripping down argument: and those that, when challenged, are referred only to the description of a desired and respected way of life, in which these moral claims have been an element essential within that way of life. The first kind of claim represents moral norms as not unlike norms of good health: the second as not unlike social customs. The issue is sharply focused by the old eighteenth-century Whig idea of the veil of ignorance: behind the veil is an abstract universal man dressed in neo-classical drapery, as in some Reynolds paintings, to indicate that he belongs to no particular place or time. In the unearthly light of the ideal, classical and timeless scene, reason cannot tell him how he should be married or how he should speak to his children or educate them or fit into his community or give one local loyalty precedence over another. For these purposes some Tory history, as in a Scott novel, has to be told of the complex conventions in which he was brought up and which fix him in a certain time and place and constitute an identity for him, so that certain moral repugnances reasonably seem to him natural to a man in his time and place and in his particular role, given the history; but certainly not natural at all times and places and in all roles.

One could clear away the obscurities of the *nature versus convention* distinction by substituting the distinction between moral claims with a requirement for convergence, for the stripping-down argument as a test, such as justice and utility, and the moral claims with no requirement for convergence and with a tendency to distinctiveness or, at least, to a licence for distinctiveness. As Plato implied, half the point of justice and the maximization of utility is lost if there is no convergence, no universal tendency, towards the cultivation of these virtues, founded on argument: not so for love and friendship and loyalty, which have their point as virtues, even if there is a chaos of different forms and different realizations of them in the world that we know.

7

Morality and Conflict

1

There is a disturbing phrase in Aristotle's definition of the human good, which (I quote) 'turns out to be activity of soul in accordance with virtue, and if there is more than one virtue, in accordance with the best and most complete.' But we must add to this 'in a complete life. For one swallow does not make a summer.' It is not difficult to understand what Aristotle is saying: the deployment of human excellence, and the most complete excellence, will only amount to happiness or well-being (*εὐδαιμονια*) if the subject's life is not amputated and if he attains the normal life-span. For happiness, in the required sense of that word, nothing must be left out and incomplete in an individual's life, neither his virtue nor his life-span. Why? Because as moral philosophers we must be looking for the perfect specimen of humanity, without defect, lacking nothing that contributes to the ideal whole person and the ideal whole life.

The idea of the human good, presented in this framework, implies that any falling away, any comparative failure in total achievement, will be a defect and a vice, a form of incompleteness: an absence of the complete human being completely active in a complete life. This is how Aristotle did in fact argue in his detailed survey of the virtues, and of virtue as a whole. A person may be deficient as a thinker, or as a practical person, as a citizen, as a politician, as a friend, all these being spheres of activity that are essential to human virtue as a whole and that are constitutive parts of it, and not merely peripheral. Aristotle does not need to deny that there are difficult questions of priority, including the famous conflict between the claims of pure thought and the claims of practical wisdom and of public life, a conflict that had been of such concern to the Platonists. The morally instructed, or wise, person strikes the right balance between conflicting interests and moral requirements at the moment of decision. With good judgement, taste and discretion, the resolution of conflicts can be found by a right ordering of the contrary tendencies in human nature. By deft calculation and educated prudence, a harmonious and complete life can be achieved, with full deployment of all the essential energies that to normal persons will most make life seem worth living. The presupposition of an attainable harmony of moral requirements is buttressed by the analogy between ethics and medicine, between the health of the soul and the health of the body. The health of the body depends upon a balance, particularly a balance in diet; similarly the health of the soul depends upon a balance. Like the life-cycle that characterizes a species of plant or an animal species, a human being has a characteristic and typical range of activities to be fitted in at the appropriate times in his life.

This analogy suggests a dubious presupposition behind the Aristotelian argument. The cycle of appropriate activities within an individual's life is being presented as a feature of the species to be properly studied by a biologist; but surely it is also a feature of particular populations whose differences are studied by historians and anthropologists? The expected stages of a complete life, from childhood through adolescence and the middle years to old age, are notoriously marked by moral requirements which are characteristic of some particular way of life, one among the many known to historians and to anthropologists. It is evident that the common sexual and reproductive needs of the species impose constraints upon the variations that are likely to be found in contrasting cultures. But history and anthropology together show that the natural constraints still leave a wide area for diversity: diversity in sexual customs, in family and kinship structures, in admired virtues appropriate to different ages and to the two sexes, in relations between social classes, also in the relation between the sexes, and in attitudes to youth and to old age. Even the notion of completeness is not free from the contamination of moral diversity; varying attitudes to old age, and to death, must modify the prevailing attitude to the completeness of a life, and to the evaluation of longevity.

The diversity in ideas of the standard complete life and of the standard pattern of admired activities, is not a merely negative phenomenon, nor is it an accidental one. The diversity is itself a primary, perhaps the primary, feature of human nature, species-wide, and it is a feature that explains many other distinguishing characteristics of the species. An analogy: it is an intrinsic feature of natural languages that they all serve to distinguish a particular group of persons within the species, and that they help to maintain the identity, and the sense of identity, of the particular group. They unite men and women, in part because they also divide them. It is part of the function of a natural language, and of the social customs and moral norms that together constitute a distinct way of life, to mark off a group of men and women, uniting the group and dividing humanity. More generally, the distinct ways of life investigated by historians and anthropologists serve to embellish and to disguise the raw and basic necessities which are common to the whole species; they are clothing for the naked creature, who unclothed can cultivate the abstract virtues which men recognize that they need in virtue of their common humanity. Men and women, adopting or conforming to a distinct way of life, realize that they have moved away from their natural condition from childhood onwards, as they become morally self-conscious within a particular style of family life and in a particular form of dependence. Not only the Garden of Eden, but many other myths, represent the transition, and represent also the common awareness of it. We therefore usually attach to the phrase 'a complete life' a content that is relative to an envisaged or actual way of life: an order of priority among different required activities and virtues, and a sequence of stages and of approved moral development.

If there is this recognized diversity in ideals of completeness, the presupposition that there is a natural and normal harmony between conflicting moral requirements becomes questionable. How could there be a guaranteed harmony among competing moral requirements and interests, a harmony founded on common human nature, if this common human nature is always overlaid by some specific moral requirements, which are not founded on a universal human nature, the naked man, and which are known to be diverse? At this point the analogy between the diversity of natural languages with their different grammars and the diversity of moral requirements for a complete life can again be invoked. It is a plausible, though still unconfirmed, hypothesis that there is a deep structure of universal grammar, determined in its turn by the needs of learning to hear, to understand, and to speak, and that this natural and universal syntax limits the diversity of historical languages. So also in the morality that governs sexuality, marriage and family relationships, it is difficult to overlook the existence of two layers of moral requirement and moral prohibition, the natural and the conventional. The dependence of very young children on adult nurture, the onset of sexual maturity, the instinctual desires associated with motherhood, the comparative helplessness of the old, are all biological features of a standard outline of human life, which may be appealed to as imposing some limits on moral requirements at all times and in all places. The precise limits may not be very definite and they may admit immense variations within the limits. But there is an argument from the natural dependence of young children to the requirement that they should be nurtured in some kind of family; or, to take account of Plato, if not in a family, that at least they should be nurtured, even if only by the state. That parents and children, or surrogate parents, have obligations and duties towards each other, requirements of reciprocal support, is also a very general moral requirement, which under challenge would probably be traced back to a natural dependence, common to the species as a whole, as well as to the distinguishing necessities of a particular way of life. What particular structure the family has, and the specific forms that the dependence and the duties of support may actually take, do vary widely with different ways of life. This two-layer account of moral requirements and of their justification implies that the universal, species-wide requirements, derived from basic human necessities, are very unspecific; they are very general restraints which are compatible with many different conceptions of the good life for men.

Some moral injunctions and prohibitions are explained and justified, when challenged, by reference to the unvarying dispositions and needs of normal human beings, living anywhere in any normal society: for example, the requirement not to cause suffering when this can be avoided. On the other hand some injunctions and prohibitions, as in duties arising from kinship, duties of politeness, of many kinds of loyalty, are in fact traced back, when challenged, to a particular way of life in which these duties are essential elements. They are essential to the way of life in the sense that they are part of an interconnected set of duties and obligations which, taken together, represent a particular and distinct moral ideal to be expressed in a distinct way of life. Men and women ordinarily know that their own way of life is one of many that have existed and that might exist. When they enter into arguments about moral issues, they often do in fact implicitly distinguish between those duties which they think they cannot neglect simply as human beings, and those duties which they think arise from a valued way of life which might, however regrettably, change radically and which might not continue forever.

2

The following moral philosophers compete with Aristotle in suggesting theoretical reconstructions of moral arguments: Hume, Kant, the utilitarians (particularly J. S. Mill and G. E. Moore), the deontologists (such as W. D. Ross and H. A. Prichard) and ideal social contract theorists (such as J. B. Rawls). This is a moderately comprehensive list of opposing moral theories, yet they are united and in agreement in one respect: their theories of moral judgement agree with Aristotle, first, in stating or implying that moral judgements are ultimately to be justified by reference to some feature of human beings which is common throughout the species; secondly, they agree with Aristotle in stating or implying that a morally competent and clear-headed person has in principle the means to resolve all moral problems as they present themselves, and that he need not encounter irresoluble problems: the doctrine of moral harmony. Admittedly Ross and Prichard did acknowledge that there occur conflicts of duties which are difficult to resolve by rational method. But their theories of moral judgement do not imply that it is unavoidable that many moral problems should be irresoluble by any constant method.

To deny the possibility of a species-wide human norm, which presents an ideal of the complete life with all the main moral requirements fulfilled, an apparently small modification of Aristotle's account of the distinguishing peculiarity of human beings is needed: he gives reason, theoretical and practical, as the peculiarity of human beings, with practical reason taking the form of deliberation both about ends and about means to ends. The other animals do not deliberate and they do not choose, at least in the special reflective way that human beings deliberate, representing to themselves, and on occasion to others, the alternatives open to them. So far Aristotle goes, but I think not far enough in distinguishing the human animal. The animals of any one species, and particularly the higher animals, often have marked characters as individuals and are often idiosyncratic in their behaviour. These differences can be accentuated by skilled breeding and by skilled training. But it remains true that it is only by inheritance, and by environmental influences, which include training, that their salient differences can be maintained and increased. They cannot be maintained by the creatures' own pleased recognition of their differences. They do not possess the power to name, and to record for themselves, the points of difference in their behaviour, and therefore they lack the power to think of these differences with pleasure or with displeasure, with pride or with shame. There is therefore a degree and a kind of expected uniformity in the behaviour over a lifetime of sub-human creatures who have similar genetic endowments and who have been subject to similar environmental influences. There will be notable individual differences. But the scope for a variety of behaviour is not indefinitely wide, and the variety is particularly limited in sexual behaviour and in family organization.

The self-conscious and willed reinforcement of differences in behaviour and in interests between groups of human beings is the effect of a shared habit of thinking of these differences historically and under descriptions that identify the differences. This source of continual reinforcement of differences is, as far as we know, unique in human beings. It is a cumulative process of differentiation between groups of human beings, who identify themselves as distinct groups by their shared and distinct natural languages and by their distinct ways of life, which are to some extent reflected in the moral vocabulary of their languages. There are many thousands of languages in the different regions of the world, and they are used to preserve the distinct history and habits of a particular population; and this remembered history will in turn reinforce the consciousness of difference.

As soon as it is recognized within moral theory that human beings reflect on their own distinguishing desires and interests, and on their own actions, in their own distinct languages, a duality opens up, which, once opened, cannot be closed; it must infect the whole of moral theory: the Greek duality between nature and convention. The distinguishing capacity for thought, which for Aristotle opened the way to a rational choice between kinds of life and kinds of human excellence, at the same time complicates and multiplies choice, and, more important, puts a limit on its rationality. As a direct consequence of the capacity to recognize and to name differences, a whole range of different complete lives is represented as normal for human beings; and the capacity to conceive these multiple alternatives is recognized as a natural power common to the whole species, alongside the power to calculate and to argue logically. Therefore the capacity to envisage conflicts between norms for a complete life, conflicts of ends and values, is natural in human beings.

Aristotle could reply that men and women are able, as thinkers, to recognize that there are many diets characteristic of different cultures; but this recognition still leaves open the question of which of these diets is best adapted to the independently determined and constant needs of human nature. As there is an ideally healthy diet for men and women of normal physique in a normal climate, should there not be a normal moral regimen correspondingly? The answer is that the power of thought makes our natural dispositions, and the natural targets of our desires, indefinitely variable in accordance with variable conceptions of these dispositions. At least this is true of those desires that are not elementary somatic impulses. The dispositions of the soul are in part constituted by reflexive thought about its dispositions, and are not exclusively to be perceived from some independent standpoint. As soon as the power of reflection develops, our so-called natural dispositions are modified by our beliefs about them, both about what they ought to be, and about their naturalness; and these beliefs are modified by the norms and ideals associated with a particular way of life, the one to which we are committed. Secondly, the ideal of health in the body is underpinned by some independent experimental knowledge of the chemical and other universal mechanisms at work in causing pain and death. We do not have, and do not expect to have, any comparable experimental knowledge of causal mechanisms in the soul; our ideals of happiness and virtue have no such underpinning.

The reinforcement of peculiarities of disposition and character, in pursuit of a distinguishing moral ideal, always entails a sacrifice of some dispositions which are greatly admired elsewhere within other ways of life. Every virtue in any particular way of life entails a specialization of powers and dispositions realized at some cost in the exclusion of other possible virtues that might be enjoyed, except that they are part of another way of life, and they cannot be grafted onto the original one. This is an ethical equivalent of the old logical principle: *omnis determinato est negatio*. As children we inherit, and may disown, a particular way of life, and a particular set of prescriptions, which specify, more or less vaguely, the expected virtues and achievements of this particular complete life. To take the Aristotelian examples: some determinate kind of justice or fairness is expected from us, as a disposition that will last a lifetime: some determinate patterns and forms of friendship and of love are expected, as a disposition, or set of dispositions, that persist through a whole life. The conflict comes from the diversification and the specialization in the forms of love and friendship taken as normal in different ways of life. I use the word 'specialization' in the sense that is sometimes given to it in popular expositions of the theory of evolution. A species of animal develops some characteristic sensory mechanism, or some characteristic type of movement, the better to escape predators, or to find food, or to select a mate in a given environment. The new power, which solves a specific problem, often entails a recognizable cost for the organism as a whole within its probable environment. A disposition to a particular form of friendship, or of love, will be at the expense of other possibilities, and will be recognized to be so. For example, the ideal of friendship between young males in some ancient Greek cities is thought to have entailed a cost in the ideal of romantic love between men and women, and perhaps also in ideals of married love, ideals that have prevailed in other places and at other times. Individuals inevitably become conscious of the cost exacted by their own way of life and of the other possibilities of achievement and enjoyment discarded. They feel the cost in internal conflict also. Every established way of life has its cost in repression.

I am not arguing for any type of ethical relativism, or that moralities cannot be compared and critized. It is a fact that a traveller, or an anthropologist, can come to understand, and can enter into and adopt, an ideal of friendship which is expressed in observances and in patterns of behaviour that were previously unknown to him. He would recognize that he had new friends, though friends of a different type, because of a close similarity in manifest sentiments of reliance and affection. He had come to understand, and to adopt, a part of an alien way of life; history shows that this quite often happens. My point is that in entering into the new norm of friendship or love he will be discarding some part of friendship or love to which he had previously subscribed; he cannot enjoy both specific forms of the virtue together.

For the other sovereign virtue, justice, the argument has to be slightly different. Justice is an abstract virtue, in the sense that a person must perceive certain definite formal relations before he knows that he has a case of justice or injustice before him. The child who exclaims 'That's not fair' has an argument of a recurrent form ready in support of his claim. For example, he will ask for an equal distribution of good things, or he will insist on some relevant difference betwen recipients which justifies an inequality. In spite of this abstract and formal identity, ideals of justice obviously differ greatly in different places and at different times in their specific content, that is, in what actions they specifically prescribe. Aristotle's ideal of justice is not difficult to understand, and his defence of it is intelligible as part of the whole way of life which he is advocating, and also as a defence specifically of justice. This way of life, and this moral ideal, have as their centre the development of superior character and superior intelligence, and a superior political organization, as the supreme priorities. Other virtues must be sacrificed to these ends, and a particular ideal of justice is required if these ends are to be obtained: unequal advantages to persons of unequal quality. In the modern liberal philosopher, J. B. Rawls, the same formal notion of justice, with its constant relation to equality, is employed to a contrary end: to prescribe that discrimination in access to primary goods should be reduced to a minimum rather than maintained, and this reduction is to be prescribed in the name of justice. The choice and pursuit of either one of these two conceptions of justice entails a cost in the loss of the values realized by the choice of the other.

It may be objected that contemporary liberal thinkers would not admit that any substantial human good is lost when the Aristotelian conception of a just society is abandoned. They may claim one conception is right and the other wrong. On this second-order question Aristotle would be in agreement: not an irresoluble conflict, but a rationally justified choice between that which is finally shown to be the correct conception and the incorrect one. A similar claim may be made for the different forms of friendship and love, though with less immediate plausibility: that one of these forms of friendship is the best or correct form, and the many others known to us are all deviations from the norm. In his two books on friendship Aristotle does argue in this way, unconvincingly, because his specific norm of friendship, in so far as Aristotle describes it, is so evidently part of one particular way of life, which is not ours, and which is not generalizable across other ways of life with their supporting virtues. Similarly the modern liberals' conception of justice in society is not generalizable as a virtue that could be imbedded in other admired ways of life without conflict with their other sustaining virtues and ideals.

3

Ways of life are sharply coherent and have their own unity in the trained dispositions that support them, and in the manners and observances and prescriptions which as children we are taught to see as normal. We learn to recognize normal conduct in the same way that we learn our native language; and not principally in the way that we learn mathematics and the law, that is, by methodical instruction, but rather by imitation. At some stage we may be introduced to a museum of normalcies which have accumulated in history. But still we cannot pick and choose bits of one picture to put besides bits of another; the coherence of the pictures comes from their distinct histories: this may be called the no-shopping principle.

There exists a multiplicity of coherent ways of life, held together by conventions and imitated habits, for much the same reasons that there is a multiplicity of natural languages, held together by conventions and imitated habits of speech. As thinking creatures we have to give meaning to our actions as satisfying certain descriptions, and there cannot be meaning without conventions, and any convention is one of an open set of possible conventions. Therefore the formation of dispositions and character, as described by Aristotle, as also the first education in Plato's *Republic*, are inadequate accounts of what actually happens in the formation of character, and inadequate accounts of what could possibly happen.

It is as if they had represented the learning of a natural language as learning the language of Adam, that is, the language which all men would speak if they had not been divided at the Tower of Babel. There is no Adamic language, and there is no set of natural dispositions which is by itself sufficient to form a normal and natural character, and to which children could be introduced. They have to learn our ways, or to learn someone's foreign or archaic ways, our forms of decent and normal living, our forms of justice and courage and friendship, or someone's alien forms. In acquiring the habits and observances, and the methods of evaluation of dispositions and character which are our methods, children are already becoming specialized as one human type among indefinitely many others. Some potentialities of their nature will never be developed, and they will usually know that; and, perhaps more important, they will feel the repression. No moralist will be able to match the physician's claim to legislate for humanity, showing a picture with the words: 'Here is the perfect moral specimen, the complete human being.'

The coherence of a way of life, and also the compatibility of the virtues cultivated within it, are clearly matters of degree. A modern, liberal, highly literate, cosmopolitan society is loosely coherent, and a secluded, pre-industrial, sub-literate community is tightly coherent, and there are many intermediate cases. Conflicts that are not easily resolved naturally occur at points of contact between two coherent sets of acknowledged virtues; again there must be uncertainty, and a sense of incompleteness and one-sidedness, which is a recognition of cost. This may typically happen when a person, or a group of persons, change their social role and are moving from one way of life to another. More radical still is the conflict that arises within an individual because his habituation within his own moral tradition has not sealed him off from alternative views of his own dispositions, as he reflects and compares. This subversive reflection may even constitute an essential part of his moral tradition, as constituting a central virtue within it: as part of a liberal tradition, already present in Pericles' speech in Thucydides. The 'no shopping' principle in its application is, once again, a matter of degree. The virtue of magnificence (*μεγαλοπρέπεια*) as specified by Aristotle, is not one that I can reasonably want to cultivate, or even can imagine cultivating, in a modern democratic society. It is a virtue that fits naturally into a coherent set of dispositions, which together constitute the moral norm for a number of aristocratic societies known in history. The 'fit' and the 'coherence' in this context are intended to stand for psychological relations, historically illustrated.

4

We are presented in the Nicomachean Ethics with two disjointed accounts, which inevitably we are unable to stitch together into a single account of the one harmonious natural life, as Aristotle intended. First, there are the essential virtues, taken as a mere list – justice, courage, temperance, practical good sense, friendship, theoretical understanding – and with a little imagination we can give them an application in our own setting, in the twentieth-century nation-state, with modern science and industry. The habits and customs that realize these dispositions are now largely different in specific detail; but we can still count the very different patterns of behaviour as expressions of the same dispositions, mapping our way of life on to Aristotle's ideal, and observing, for instance, that we still admire and praise genuine knowledge as Aristotle praised contemplation (*θεωρία*). The second, and disjointed, aspect of the Nicomachean Ethics is the very specific Greek ideal of the free citizen, the man of leisure, prepared to participate in the government of his city, cultivating his intelligence, a leader in his society, rightly deferred to by the lower orders, by slaves and by non-citizens, manly and consciously superior to women, who are dependent on men, respecting always differences of quality among persons and respecting the status that properly attaches to these differences. This disjointedness between the two aspects of the Nicomachean Ethics, the abstract and the specific, is not to be remedied, because to name the virtues is not to describe specific patterns of behaviour, nor to describe the specific thoughts and feelings that support the behaviour; the character of a person, or even of a type of person, is not sufficiently represented by such abstract terms, and the value and nobility, or the mere decency, of his way of living is not to be recognizably reproduced at this level of abstraction. In so far as Aristotle does describe specifically the morally ideal person and the morally normal life, there emerges a person and a way of life which are very far from the ordinary moral opinions (*τὰἔνδοξα*) which now prevail in the industrial West and which support a largely different way of life. Aristotle inserts an ideal, a balance in virtue between, for example, practical and theoretical activities, and which was demanded by the nature of the mind and of its faculties, as a balance in diet is demanded by our bodies. But happiness and fulfilment are not analogous to health, as this ideal of balance requires. If Wittgenstein was, on reflection, happy that he had devoted his life to philosophy at the expense of other possibilties, as it is recorded that he was, it cannot be true that he ought for his own good to have aimed at complete virtue, in the Aristotelian sense of a balance of virtues, including the practical and political virtues.

My argument repeatedly returns to this starting-point: that the capacity to think scatters a range of differences and conflicts before us: different languages, different ways of life, different specializations of aim within a way of life, different conventions and styles also within a shared way of life, different prohibitions. A balanced life is a particular moral ideal to which there reasonably can be, and have been, alternatives acceptable to thoughtful men at different times and places: not only to Gauguin and Flaubert, the usual examples, but to men and women following specialized ways of life at different places and times: following ideals of courage and endurance, ideals of altruism and social service, ideals of detachment and contemplation, an ideal of maintaining a family tradition, ideals of science and learning – all of these abstractly-named ideals have been embodied as elements in admired ways of life, and there are certainly many others. Those who have been governed by one of these ideals, or by two or more of them in a lifetime, have experienced conflict in themselves and have seen moral conflict all around them. They always knew that there were alternatives, and that they have adopted, or they had been born into and had not rejected, a way of life which excluded other virtues no less well known to thoughtful men and women. They knew that there had been, and would be, many other admirable ways of living even if they also thought, as they often did, that their arrangement of priorities was the best.

Our everyday and raw experience is of a conflict between contrary moral requirements at every stage of almost anyone's life: why then should moral theorists – Kantians, utilitarians, deontologists, contractarians – look for an underlying harmony and unity behind the facts of moral experience? Why should there be a residuary Platonism here, even today, when Platonism has lost its hold in the theory of knowledge? The Nicomachean Ethics suggest one answer at one level, the rational level, for the persistence of a partial Platonism, even among those who, like Aristotle, think that they have escaped from Plato. The phrase 'the things that admit of being otherwise' (*τὰἐνδεχομενα ἀλλωςἐχειν*) are still not for Aristotle proper objects of the purest and most elevated and most honourable kind of thought, which is concerned with things that must be as they are, and that clearly could not be otherwise. This evaluative proposition about thought and knowledge is the fundamental tenet of Platonism; there is a deep structure of knowable necessity behind contingent appearances. Throughout the Nicomachean Ethics Aristotle is trying to show that practical reason is respectably systematic and methodical, and truly deserves its name of reason, within the limits set by the irreducible particularity and contingency of actual situations. There is a similar desire to exhibit a rational structure behind the superficial contingency of moral requirements in Kant, in the utilitarians and in ideal contract theory. If a practice, or an institution, an obligation or a duty or a right, is said to exist by convention, it is implied that things could have been otherwise. Anything that is a matter of convention and admits of alternatives will have a historical explanation. It cannot be part of the necessary structure of reality, to which reason in its most elevated employment can penetrate. Aristotle's ambition in the Nicomachean Ethics is to show the deep structure, the foundation in nature, the 'why' of our ordinary moral beliefs. Many different sets of clothes conventionally covering the same body, the natural object beneath, will all reveal something of the structure of the body. We can therefore neglect the superficial diversity of actual moral beliefs and practices, attributing this diversity to the contingency of changing social conditions producing diverse social customs. Beneath the social customs there is a solid structure of moral necessity, and the moral necessities are of overriding importance, while the social customs are comparatively trivial in the demands that they make on us.

If this picture is correct, the conflicts that we actually experience in plumping for one way of life with its customs are either signs of muddled thinking or they are superficial conflicts, clashes between different cultures and customs only, and not deep ultimate moral conflicts, to be taken with all the seriousness implied by the word 'moral' in contrast with the words 'custom' and 'convention'. Within the single, fully admirable way of life there will be difficult decisions, conflicts between values all of which ought to be included in the complete life, and hence there will be trade-offs. But these admissions fall far short of my claim that there must always be moral conflicts which cannot, given the nature of morality, be resolved by any constant and generally acknowledged method of reasoning. My claim is that morality has its sources in conflict, in the divided soul and between contrary claims, and that there is no rational path that leads from these conflicts to harmony and to an assured solution, and to the normal and natural conclusion.

There are the famous sentences and phrases in the Nicomachean Ethics where Aristotle seems about to turn away from Plato's ghost. They are the sentences about perception (*ἐντῃαἰσθησει ἥκρισις*) and about the observation of the particular circumstances of the particular case being all-important. But the whole framework of the Ethics, in Books I, VI and X, holds Aristotle fast, and he does not escape from the old gradings of thought and of knowledge, as in the divided line of the Republic. There is a snobbery of abstract thought at the expense of perception of the contingent, of the concrete, of the particular, of the historical accident, of the objects of the presumed lower reaches of the mind. It is as if the theory of aristocracy, and of necessary social gradation, had been transferred to the theory of knowledge.

Learning a language, and speaking and understanding and writing a language, are typical thoughtful activities, and typical exercises of intelligence. The kinds of precision, and the kinds of clarity, required are different from those required in mathematics, and each of these exercises of intelligence present their own kind of difficulty. There is also the difference that the structures of mathematics to be learnt, and their uses to be elaborated, are everywhere the same, not confined to particular places and times; there is a history of their discovery, but they do not otherwise have a history, unlike the structures of languages, which all have a history and which are best explained and understood through their history. This is not the place to assess the worth and dignity of the study of history and of languages as yielding forms of knowledge; but it is certain that the conventions of behaviour and of sentiment that enter into our moralities have to be understood by reference to their history, as also do the specific divergences between different ways of life. Against Plato, Oscar Wilde can be quoted: 'It is only shallow people who do not judge by appearances', and he meant by 'appearances' surfaces, the direct objects of perception, including styles of expression.

That the conventions governing sexual customs and family relationships, and the forms of personal respect and good manners, may greatly vary is no reason for concluding that the morality of sexuality and family is superficial in a person's life, at least if superficial entails unimportant, or even that manners and styles of expression are unimportant. We know that in the average life nothing is more important in moral consciousness than family and sexual relations, and than love and friendship, and their accepted manners of expression also. That which is very variable in human relations, determined by transient habits and social forms and easily susceptible of being otherwise, may have profound moral importance, alongside universal principles of justice and utility. Not only that: but a perception of the variability and of the contingency, even of the merely accidental nature, of a moral prohibition, often in fact contributes to our sense of its importance. When Flaubert and Proust paid most careful attention to the uses of the past imperfect tense in French, they knew that they were concerned with a surface feature of one language and of one literature. But Proust's observations on the uses of the past tense in Flaubert made a point which was also important for literature and language in general, and he knew that it was. Similarly, paying attention to a mode of address, a sexual prohibition, a family ritual, a style of communication between employee and employer, a custom among friends, may be a case of paying attention to an institution that is characteristic of a particular way of life at a particular time, or of the moral character of a particular person who has adopted or inherited a particular way of life. The understanding of these institutions as parts of a way of life is one route to the understanding of morality in general. Certain minutiae of behaviour, as they strike a stranger, may be emblematic and have the right or wrong emotional significance for those who understand the behaviour, 'understand' in the sense that one understands an idiom in a spoken language.

When the ancient picture is challenged along these lines, the metaphor of superficial and variable contrasted with deep and constant loses its application to morality. Each way of life shows in its regulations a characteristic design and direction. We expect there to be a recognizable vision of humanity and of its particular possibilities, a vision that animates the particular system of moral rules, however transient the vision, now preserved only in a surviving literature or painting. The same rule of politeness which in one way of life may be a triviality of social custom, of no moral significance, may have a significant place in another way of life, marking mutual respect between persons, which is a general moral necessity, differently reflected in wholly different conduct.

5

I am not arguing for moral relativism, taken as the thesis that ways of life, with their priorities among virtues and their dependent moral rules, are not subjects for moral judgement, because there is no independent ground from which they can be evaluated. On the contrary, there are several ways in which they can be judged and ought to be judged: not only may a way of life fail actually to satisfy the purposes, and to permit the virtues, which it purports to satisfy and to permit, and be internally incoherent; but it may also lead to the destruction of life and to greater misery and degradation and to gross injustice, as Nazism did. These are always and everywhere considerations that count for evil in striking the balance between good and evil. There are obvious limits set by common human needs to the conditions under which human beings flourish and human societies flourish. History records many ways of life which have crossed these limits. Rather I have argued that human nature, conceived in terms of common human needs and capacities, always underdetermines a way of life, and underdetermines an order of priority among virtues, and therefore underdetermines the moral prohibitions and injunctions that support a way of life. I am making three points against the classical moralists: (a) that there cannot be such a thing as the complete human good; nor (b) can there be a harmony among all the essential virtues in a complete life; nor (c) can we infer what is universally the best way of life from propositions about human nature. Human nature includes the capacity to reflect on, and compare, aims and ideals, and to reflect on this reflection, which in turn demands the capacity to evolve conventions of behaviour alongside linguistic conventions, and thereby to create a moral order within the natural order. Whether it is Aristotelian, Kantian, Humean, or utilitarian, moral philosophy can do harm when it implies that there ought to be, and that there can be, fundamental agreement on, or even a convergence in, moral ideals – the harm is that the reality of conflict, both within individuals and within societies, is disguised by the myth of humanity as a consistent moral unit across time and space. There is a false blandness in the myth, an aversion from reality. We know that we in fact have essential divisions within us as persons and that we experience moral conflicts arising from them. A person hesitates between two contrasting ways of life, and sets of virtues, and he has to make a very definite, and even final, determination between them. This determination is a negation, and normally the agent will feel that the choice has killed, or repressed, some part of him.

Similarly in the public domain: for example, we know that accelerating natural science and technology often produces effects that are morally ambiguous and uncertain and that they import drastic changes into cherished and admired ways of life. An appeal to the alleged constancies of human nature, to the fixed array of natural powers and to universal virtues, will not represent our natural way of thinking about such problems. The effects of new science and of new technology on ideals of work, on family relations, on local loyalties, and on norms of intelligence and on education, cannot be thought about effectively at a level highly abstracted from historical realities. We have both to perceive and to imagine the effects developing within one, or more, actual ways of life which we understand, and to confront the concrete decisions which force a determination between them.

Not all moral determinations are matters of balance; there is also unmixed evil. The Nazis tried to establish a way of life which entirely discarded justice and gentleness, among many other generally recognized virtues, and they deliberately made the claim 'anything goes' under these headings. The claim 'anything goes' is a sign of evil, because it calls for the destruction of the human world of customary moral claims precariously established within the setting of natural human interests. An uncritical Machiavellianism, or an uncritical consequentialism such as Lenin's, or that of subsequent communist and Fascist leaders, may extend the claim 'anything goes' across several of the virtues, draining past ways of life of their value, without a compensating vision of new virtues in a new way of life. The Nazis repudiated justice, and they dismissed considerations of utility and benevolence; they also undermined most of the moral conventions of their society. There is a kind of moral dizziness that goes with such destruction of conventional restraints and of normal decencies in social relations. Because we do not altogether understand why the restraints have developed in precisely the way that they have, we respond with moral anxiety and shock to the cry 'anything goes'. The normal decencies of behaviour evidently might have been different from what they are, if the relevant history had been different. The contingency of the rules does not detract from their stringency: on the contrary, a consciousness of the contingency, a belief that the rules could have been different, with the constancies of human nature remaining the same, tends to reinforce the shared sense that the rule must not be broken, except for an overriding consideration; to break it is to undermine morality more generally. The analogy between linguistic rules and moral rules helps to explain this stringency. The more idiomatic a usage is, whether of grammar or of vocabulary, the more disturbing or absurd is the impression made by a failure to follow the usage. One shows oneself to be a foreigner and a stranger with particular vividness if one's pronunciation of a word is in accordance with consistency and logic, but is at variance with the correct pronunciation, which is usually determined by historical accident as much as by consistency. Every natural language flaunts its idioms and inconsistencies, because they lend the language, spoken and written, its distinctive flavour and spirit. In some important areas of morality, which are the least regulated by rational calculation, the rules that support the distinctive features of a particular way of life, and its determinate conception of the human good, will be particularly stringent rules.

Stringency, necessity: these are the notions that we associate with moral injunctions and prohibitions. Most duties and obligations present themselves as conflicts. Sometimes an individual can present, in a rational reconstruction, the argument that made one final conclusion necessary. This is the Aristotelian picture of practical reason, and it fits many occasions of private life in which utilities are to be calculated, and in which justice as fairness is at stake. This Aristotelian picture even more evidently fits many occasions in public life. Typical difficulties in politics arise when considerations of justice and utility come into conflict. Those who are responsible in politics generally have to be in a position to give a persuasive justificatory account of their decisions to those who are affected by them. Aristotle expressly modelled his account of rational choice on public political debate. But there are many occasions in normal life, particularly in personal relations, when a course of action presents itself as morally necessary, and any alternative as morally impossible, and yet nothing like a clear account could be given of the factors that make the action necessary. If the agent reflects, he will say: 'The necessity is not principally a matter of reason, in the sense of calculation; it is more a matter of reflective feeling and of perception, and of a feeling and a perception which I am prepared to stand by and to endorse.'

The standard objection to accepting the appeal to feeling and to perception is that it is a dangerous form of irrationalism, opening the way to prejudice and bigotry. But it is not irrational not to rely on explicit reasoning and calculation in spheres in which the empirical premisses required for the reasoning are known to be, or are likely to be, extremely unclear and indefinite, or difficult to analyse. An action or a policy may be felt to be, or perceived to be, squalid, or mean, or disloyal, or dishonourable, even though the agent can give no very precise and explicit account of why on this particular occasion he perceives the situation in this light. He may be sure that the action or policy has to be rejected as unworthy and repugnant, reasonably trusting his reflective feelings about it, which may have arisen because he has noticed features of the situation that he does not know that he has noticed and that he cannot spell out and analyse. Secondly, the contrast between reason and emotion, derived from the old faculty psychology, is not a clear contrast. There are considered and thoughtful mental attitudes, accompanied by strong feeling, which typically come into conflict with each other in difficult moral situations. We have no exact science that can be applied to the study of human feeling, and of admiration and respect and remorse and sense of loss. The usual models of practical reasoning are often too definite to be applicable: the fitting of a particular instance under a general principle, as in law, or the fitting of means to ends, as in engineering. We need not in moral matters aspire always to reason in a scientific style, when the issue is not one of probable consequence, or of articulated law and justice. In some matters of serious moral concern, we ought not to pretend to reason like engineers and technicians and lawyers, or even like doctors, who sometimes have a tested body of knowledge to deploy in their practical syllogisms.

6

A stable feature of human nature, over and above a normal physical constitution, is the need to possess a distinct history, which is one's own and not that of all mankind, and also to cultivate that which is particular and that is believed to be the best of this time and of that place, alongside and within the universal moral claims that are common to all people as such. In difficult decisions involving conflicts, people are being required to determine what their overriding moral commitments are, and what their priorities are among the activities and achievements that they value in their lives. They are always throwing away something that they value, or at least that they have thought that they valued. If they are average morally sensitive persons, they know that they have failed to respond to moral claims which they had always believed were binding; but they could not have anticipated the contingencies of their experience, in which they found that they could not combine loyalty to all the interests, and all the values, which they had believed make life worth living. As they grow older, they will normally perceive that they are going lop-sided to the grave.

This point about moral conflict can be made by contrasting moral requirements with ordinary, morally neutral ambitions and desires. There is no incoherence in the idea that a person might in a lifetime realize every morally insignificant ambition and strong desire which he has had. The supposition is unlikely often to be true, but it cannot be ruled out *a priori* as incoherent. In retrospect, one comments on one's good luck; circumstances had never imposed the choice between two strong desires and tastes. Why then should a man or woman not be rightly described as having led a morally blameless life, in the sense that they had never rejected a serious moral claim made upon them, having been fortunate in not encountering the worst kind of moral conflict? Clearly these words could be used and they would be understood, and they might even convey a truth, rightly interpreted. But to have a fortunately blameless life, in this negative sense, is not the same as having the best possible life, in a moral sense. The blameless subject would not say of himself that he *happened* only to admire, and to intend to cultivate, only those virtues which in his conduct he had shown himself to possess; and he happened also to be uninterested in all other ways of life, with their supporting virtues, except his own. A person's morality cannot be a matter of what he happens to admire, or believe in, as a matter of psychological fact; but he can, if he chooses, accept his desires and tastes, in so far as he regards them as morally insignificant, as just matters of fact. If a person has lived a blameless life 'according to his lights', as the saying goes, the question always arises – 'Were his lights good enough, or could they have been better?'; and this question arises for him as agent, as he knows, no less than for unkind observers. For this reason the phrase 'a blameless life' is very far from being enthusiastic praise of a person. It suggests confined purposes and an absence of enterprise and absence of larger views. Even persons exclusively committed to one clearly delineated way of life, which they are sure is the only right one, ought to admit, if they reflect, that the virtues that they cultivate, and the moral claims that they act on, both entail a cost; even though they are sure that the cost ought to be paid. If they think, like Aristotle, that effective action in public affairs is part of the best way of life, then they will admit that total candour is excluded for them. The Chancellor of the Exchequer is not required to respond honestly to questions about a future devaluation of the currency.

I am not merely arguing the case for the plurality of values, and the impossibility of realizing all positive values in a single life, a case that has been persuasively argued by Isaiah Berlin, among others. My thesis entails the plurality, but it is a stronger thesis and differently grounded. Belief in the plurality of values is compatible with the belief that the different and incompatible values are all eternally grounded in the nature of things, and, more specifically, in human nature. Then Aristotle was in error in supposing ultimate conflicts to be in principle, and with luck, avoidable. But still a definite list of essential virtues, deducible from human nature alone, could be drawn up, even if there will always be conflicts between them; and I deny that such a list is possible. My claim rests on the indispensable and related notions of convention and ways of life, and on the analogy between moralities and natural languages in respect of their plurality; and this analogy, I am claiming, is more than superficial. Just as we know that each of the many natural languages evolves, and that linguistic conventions of grammar and idiom change with changing circumstances, so also the moral conventions that support a particular way of life change.

The attainment of complete virtue, and of the human good deducible from human nature, have been postponed in the theories of philosophers of history in the last century, particularly by Marx and Comte. Historical development, rationally managed, will lead upwards and on to a final perfection. The partial moralities and partial satisfactions of the past should be redeemed in a final stage, in which the potentialities of humanity are realized in full in a final social adjustment. Many reasons have been given in the last few decades for rejecting this linear and teleological view of historical development as ungrounded and not credible. If my thesis about morality is correct, a teleological theory of human development in any form entails an impossibility, the impossibility of human perfection and of the full realization of all human potentialities. We may compare and reasonably praise or condemn past and present established ways of life by reference to their consequences for human welfare, and by standards of justice and fairness which we can defend by argument, even if there are no rigorous proofs in this kind of argument. We can make similar, though less fundamental, comparisons between languages in respect of their clarity in communication and of their potentialities in literature, or between legal systems by reference to general standards of equity and clarity. Just as there is no reason to regard all, or any, natural language as an approximation to, or a partial realization of, the ultimate, perfect language, so there is every reason not to think of past and present ways of life, with their supporting and dominant virtues, as phases in the development towards the one perfect way of life.

There is an implication for political thought: we ought not to plan for a final reconciliation of conflicting moralities in a perfect social order; we ought not even to expect that conflicts between moralities, which prescribe different priorities, will gradually disappear, as rational methods in the sciences and in law are diffused. We know virtually nothing about the factors determining the ebb and flow of moral beliefs, conventions and commitments; and we know very little about the conditions under which an intense and exclusive attachment to a particular way of life develops, as opposed to a more selective and critical attitude to the moral conventions that prevail in the environment. We are still in the dark about the dominant phenomenon in contemporary politics: nationalism.

We ordinarily recognize that many moral claims that we accept are to be explained by the history of a particular person or population, and they provoke the question 'Why is this prescription a binding one, given that evidently this moral claim is not to be accepted as valid for all mankind?' There is often no fully rational answer either of Durkheimian form, pointing to the bad consequences of disregarding established conventions, except when they are harmful; or, alternatively, of the functional kind, which might show that the specific practices enjoined contribute to an independently approved goal. Within a particular convention of behaviour that prevails in a particular population, a set of actions and reactions which, within conventions prevailing elsewhere, might be repugnant, might here be natural and acceptable. The social context, formed by interlocking conventions, generally makes all the difference to the perception and assessment of types of conduct, which perhaps could be described from a neutral standpoint as identical. There is the analogous fact that there are acceptable and admirable ways of applying paint to canvas within the conventions of abstract expressionism which would be unacceptable within the conventions of Renaissance painting.

I must repeat, to avoid misunderstanding, that strict reasoning, both computational and quasi-legal, certainly has an immense part in moral thought, particularly in public affairs and, more specifically still, in problems of peace and war. Very often, though not universally and necessarily, rational considerations of human welfare and of justice override, and ought to override, all more intuitive perceptions of the value of particular relationships and practices and sentiments. But when we do discard conventions of behaviour, or even whole ways of life, on moral grounds that are fully explicit and rational, we shall unavoidably find ourselves entering into other conventions and into another way of life. We shall not find ourselves, as the Enlightenment philosophers hoped, citizens of the world, unclothed in the sole light of reason, computing what is best for mankind as a whole, or computing abstract justice, and guided by no considerations of another less rational kind. If persons do pursue an ideal of pure rationality, such as the one recommended by the utilitarians, they will find that they are disguising from themselves the moral considerations that explain much of their own conduct; these considerations can be classified as moral, because they engage reflective feelings of respect and admiration, or remorse and repugnance. A rational moralist will retort that, as things are, he will be struggling against his upbringing and against ordinary social influences in following his rational morality. And it is this struggle between reason and sentiment that is the essence of morality, he will claim; and the advocacy of a rational morality, whether by a utilitarian or by a Kantian, is a statement of what ought to be, and not a description of the actual state of our unreformed moralities, which are tainted by social custom and by inherited dispositions. I am arguing against such a rational moralist that reason both is, and ought to be, not the slave of the passions in practical matters, but the equal partner of the passions, when these are circumscribed as the reflective passions.

Hume's enlightened theory of moral reasoning can be criticized at two points: first, he accepts a simple and sharp dichotomy between reason, which is calculative reason, and passion and desire, which move to action; and this leaves no clear place for the wide range of reflective thought and judgement which does not consist of explicit calculation and argument. Secondly, Hume argues that nature has so designed us that we tend towards agreement and harmony in moral questions, if we have normal sentiments and sympathies. I have been arguing that nature has so designed us that, taking humanity as a whole and the evidences of history, we tend to have conflicting and divergent moralities imbedded in divergent ways of life, each the product of specific historical memories and local conditions. If a person disclaimed any commitment to any set of conventions, he would lack the normal means of conveying his feelings, and of responding to the feelings of others through shared discriminations and evaluations. Mathematics and the natural sciences do cross frontiers and unite humanity. But we also need to enter into, and to share, the conventions of significant behaviour and of speech and of expression which hold a community together as a community, in part thereby creating the frontier which is crossed by mathematics and the natural sciences.

There is a further ground for not rejecting, in the name of reason, moral divergence and moral conflict over and above the values of diversity and individuality, and also the value of community. It is a consideration, mentioned in chapter 1, that is not easily made clear. We stand to the natural order, within which we know ourselves to be a subordinate part, as scientific observers of nature and as manipulators of it in the service of our own interests. There is nothing to prevent our studying ourselves, and studying human beings generally, as natural objects which function in accordance with regularities and laws that we find to be universal, or at least general, in nature. We can apply this natural knowledge to change our own physical and mental states and our dispositions in desired and approved directions. We are also apt to adopt towards the natural order, including human nature, an altogether different stance. We decorate it, play variations upon it for our pleasure, disguise it and cover it, enhance it, and leave a personal or communal mark upon it. We enclose, and set boundaries, to parts of the natural environment, not only for use, but for pleasure. As the clearest, concrete example of this attitude to nature, Kant cited gardens, and, more particularly, the English landscape garden of the eighteenth century.

The symbolism of gardens in literature is extensive and old, and I shall not pursue it here. It is at least clear that a garden is a celebration of nature by means of embellishing it and of constraining it for the sake of pleasure. A garden is intended to be a fusion of naturalness and of artificiality, created for the sake of the pleasure and of the reassurance that this fusion brings. Secondly, the shapes and forms of any satisfactory garden show the conventions of the particular type to which the garden belongs, and each type has a history and a sentimental significance. We constrain a tract of nature, unclothed, to take on forms which have a known history and which show human invention. We humanize a landscape and an environment in this way and, having lent it a visible history, we are able to feel at home in it. Another relevant example of the embellishment and enhancing of nature in accordance with variable conventions, which have a history, has already been mentioned: the adornment of the body with clothes. Clothes, whether sophisticated or primitive, play variations upon the human body and its shape. They convey both sexual and social ideas, and are linked in several ways to sexuality, as sexuality is conventionally developed and restrained in a particular population. Much clothing is not directly functional, but rather is designed to be pleasing, and usually also to suggest a social role. Approved clothing can be at once capricious and conventional. One would be amazed if one found a people who had no conventions governing the covering or the decoration of their bodies.

Just as there is no ideally rational arrangement of a garden, and no ideally rational clothing, so there is no ideally rational way of ordering sexuality and there is no ideally rational way of ordering family and kinship relationships. The ordering is subject to rational control, specifically in respect of the comparative fairness or unfairness of the arrangements and of their tendency under particular conditions to promote happiness or harm. These are the arguable matters, and the arguments can cross frontiers when comparisons between different whole ways of life are made. Within the limits of our biological nature, and restrained by rational calculation of consequences and of fairness within a group or population, we invent our sexual second nature, usually as customs of a particular community; and the customs that constitute a type of family, and a kinship structure, are a second nature also, an embellishment of the naked, biological man, carrier of genes. As raw food has to be cooked and changed in accordance with learnt custom, natural sexuality also has to be trimmed and directed in accordance with some customs or other. When ideally natural arrangements are sought in, for example, clothing or in sexual practices, the result is one more fashion, later seen as characteristic of a particular period and of a particular place.

Christian marriage is one institution among others, entailing a large number of moral claims for those who accept the institution, or accept some variant of it, as part of their way of life. Christian marriage itself has a long history of changing moral claims and virtues – for example, the claims of romantic love, of fidelity, of chastity, of responsible paternity and maternity, of the sharing of property. Whatever choices a man or woman may make among all the variants under these headings, they will be entering into an interconnected set of duties and obligations, many of which are not to be explained and justified by utilitarian calculations; nor as deducible from Kantian imperatives binding on all rational persons; nor adequately justified as instances of justice and fairness. It remains true that we balance, and must always balance, the calculable requirements of justice and utility against the uncalculated requirements of reflective moral sentiment; and neither side, the universal or the customary, can be known *a priori* to be always and in all circumstances overriding.

7

The word 'institution' must finally come into the discussion because all men and women belong to, or are imbedded in, some institutions, which impose moral claims on them. It is not enough to follow the current habit among moral philosophers who write about 'practices' as distinct from individual actions. An institution is a more formally established, and a more definitely identifiable, entity than a practice; it is generally governed by its own observances and rituals. The moral claims of pure practical reason, calculating consequences, often come into conflict with the duties and obligations that arise from participation in an institution, and there sometimes is no third, independent source of moral arbitration.

The old question arises once again: would it not be better, as a policy for an enlightened and reformed way of life, to subject every institution around us, and every loyalty thereby engendered, to constant rational scrutiny and criticism? If the institution serves a useful purpose from the standpoint of human happiness, or from the standpoint of a just order of things, then its moral claims can be endorsed; if not, not. Marriage as an institution, with its present obligations and rituals, can be evaluated from this double standpoint of utility and justice, and the validity of a range of moral claims would be thereby rationally tested. Has it not already been admitted that we must always evaluate moral claims, and even a whole way of life, by reference to human welfare and to justice as fairness? It is easy to think of institutions loyally preserved, and of whole ways of life long sustained, which have been cruel and oppressive and grossly unjust in their effects, and which ought for these reasons to have been destroyed, and their moral claims repudiated. They were prolonged by a lack of rational criticism, by respect for tradition and for the past, and by an inert moral conservatism.

A distinction needs to be made to meet this objection: there is a large difference, and a logical independence, between two moral philosophies, often confused. First, there is a moral philosophy that prescribes rational evaluation of moral claims and institutions and that in normal circumstances prescribes the rejection of moral claims and institutions which damage human welfare or which are unjust in their operation; but there sometimes are overriding considerations when the damage caused is not too great and the injustice too extreme and when the opposing values are far from trivial. This moral philosophy, defended here, asserts that there always will be, and that there always ought to be, conflicts between moral requirements arising from universal requirements of utility and justice, and moral requirements that are based on specific loyalties and on conventions and customs of love and friendship and family loyalty, historically explicable conventions. The second moral philosophy asserts that any moral claim is finally valid if and only if it either contributes to human welfare or promotes justice; there is a double criterion which should solve conflicts by entirely rational argument, except when justice and utility conflict. For the second philosophy the only finally acceptable conflict is between utility and justice, the two universal requirements which all reasonable persons must acknowledge. The first moral theory asserts that moral conflicts are of their nature ineliminable and that there is no morally acceptable and overriding criterion, simple or double, to be appealed to, and no constant method of resolving conflicts. Moral considerations are an open set, new ones arise, and old ones disappear, in the natural course of history. The worth and value of a person's life and character, and also of a social structure, are always underdetermined by purely rational considerations.

Many of the moral claims that persons recognize are changed or modified as time passes; but their dispositions and moral beliefs ought to be reasonably consistent over time; and they would be ashamed if there were too many abrupt moral conversions, with their own past repudiated.

They recognize moral claims that arise from the requirement that their lives, or some considerable part of their lives, should exhibit some consistency of aim and some coherent character. An explanation of the moral claims would have to be, partly at least, historical, referring to their past and their consciousness of the past. As for persons, so for institutions; they also need some continuity, if their individuality as distinct entities is to be preserved; their history ideally has to make sense as the story of something that had a well-defined character, while it existed, a character of its own. Loyalty is only one of the virtues that derives its necessity from the necessity of continuity, and of continuity through change. A person's family, father and more, origins, and ancestors, in so far as a person knows who they were, contribute to the picture that the person forms of his own nature and place in the world. This place in the world defines some of the obligations and duties. He will probably have reasons for trying to change his nature and place in the world; but the emotional involvement, through conscious and unconscious memories, to some degree ties him or her to the past, and particularly to family relationships, as he sees them. Therefore any person, man and woman alike, will be interested both in explaining and in justifying their present conduct by referring to their personal history. Historical explanation, as a mode of understanding, comes naturally to everyone, because all normal men and women are interested in their own origins and their own history and the history of their family. They are not able to think of themselves, as utilitarians and Kantians demand, as unclothed citizens of the universe, merely rational and 'sentient' beings, deposited in no particular place at no particular time.

Conventions; moral perceptions and feelings; institutions and loyalties; tradition; historical explanations – these are related features, and ineliminable features, of normal thought about the conduct of life and about the character and value of persons. In theoretical reasoning there are two elements which are analogous to the universal considerations and the conventional considerations in practical reason. These are the methodology of the natural sciences, based on experiment and on quantitative methods, and directed towards the discovery of universal laws, and the methodology of the humanities, specifically history and the study of languages and literatures, based on informed critical judgement of the evidence and on the interpretation of texts. Trying to undermine Descartes' theory of knowledge, with its paradigms of knowledge in mathematics and physics, Vico claimed in *La Scienza Nuova* that there exists also a human world created by men in the course of their development towards full humanity. This is the world of natural languages and of their grammars, of law and legal institutions, of art and poetry and fiction, of social structures, such as republics and monarchy, slavery and aristocracy. The discipline that is the study of this man-made world he called philology. We must use the methods that we use in interpreting languages also in interpreting the laws and legal institutions, the customs, the social structures, and also the poetry and fiction, of the past. According to Vico, because every person has developed in thought and feeling from childhood into full adult rationality, he can, through memory, imaginatively enter into the ages of poetry, with their accompanying social structures, when history, or the history of a particular people, records the childhood of humanity. As microcosms within the macrocosm of history, we can recall the transition from the imaginative, inventive, emotionally unrestrained thoughts and feelings of childhood to the controlled rationality of adults, who are guided principally by concepts and calculations and are not guided, like children, principally by images and fantasies. History is not simply inferior as knowledge to science; it has its own kind of assurance, because we can in fact imaginatively recapture the meaning and spirit of institutions and of languages and literatures which are long past and foreign to us. We can understand them as human inventions, because we have all engaged in similar inventions in our own time. Men and women are influenced by the historical notion of legitimacy. They consequently look for the foundation of their present conduct in the conventions and institutions within which their family and their forebears lived. Social institutions and moral conventions, like the conventions of literature and of art, and the conventions of speech, need all to be understood and evaluated as phases of human development. Vico insists that that which is of great value in one phase of thought cannot be successfully reproduced and imitated in a different phase of thought, and cannot be just transplanted from one way of life to another, as the results of natural science can be: the no-shopping principle again.

A rational explanation, answering a 'why?' question, is always a case of exhibiting a multiplicity of particular cases as falling under a comparatively simple principle or rule: the more simple, the better the explanation. There is a very substantial part of morality, and of moral concern, which requires the recognition of complexity and not the reduction of complexity to simplicity. Consider a typical intersection of the two kinds of moral thinking: a person may ask – 'Is not this sexual and family custom unjust, and therefore to be condemned?' Argument might show that the custom does offend against some entirely general principles of fairness and justice, and this is a very strong ground for condemning it. But the custom might be one of a network of interconnected customary family relationships which could not be radically disturbed without undermining a whole valued way of life. In a particular case, involving individuals and their particular circumstances, the general considerations about justice might reasonably be thought less weighty and action-inducing than complex features of the situation which could not easily and naturally be expressed in general terms, even less reduced to general principles. At any time, and particularly, but not solely, in private life, the practical need is often for sensitive observation of the easily missed features of the situation, not clear application of principles. There is no overriding reason why we should look for simplicity, clarity and exactness in the conduct of life, or in every aspect of the conduct of life, as we do look for them in scientific explanation. We have no pressing need for satisfactory total explanations of our conduct and of our way of life. Our need is rather to construct and maintain a way of life of which we are not ashamed and which we shall not, on reflection, regret or despise, and which we respect. Our thinking generally is, and always ought to be, directed to this end, being practical and imaginative rather than an expression of theoretical curiosity. The repugnant aspect of utilitarianism is its ambition to explain everything, and to find a formula which will circumscribe permissible human concerns, once and for all.

There is a further – and last – possible misunderstanding of my thesis. If one stresses the unrationalized balancing of competing moral claims as characteristic of moral thinking, there is the risk that the word 'balance' will leave a too comfortable impression: as if one lives within morality, and within the moral conventions of a particular society, as within a stable building with secure foundations. In this century it is impossible to preserve this picture of stability. It has been obvious that respect for justice, and also any morality founded on concern for human welfare, are fragile constructions, liable to be toppled at any time by cruelty and fanaticism, and by the will to power. Alongside the balancing of conflicting moral claims, thinking about morality also includes thinking how barriers against evil are most reliably maintained: that is, about how a standard of bare decency in social arrangements is to be maintained; for this standard is always under threat. This thinking about social evils is not generally a matter of the judicious balancing of competing moral claims, but rather of expressing and eliciting strong moral feelings. As morality is inextricably involved with conflict, so also it is inextricably involved with the control of destructive impulses. If morality were to be defined, which is unnecessary, it might be defined by reference to its central topics, and not by the alleged logical peculiarities of moral judgements, in the manner of Kant. It is a system of prohibitions and injunctions concerning justice in social relations, the control of violence and of killings of all kinds, about war and peace, the regulation of kinship, the customs of friendship and family. My argument has been that it is for us natural to be unnatural in these spheres, following both reason and history, and consequently it is natural for us to be involved in repression and conflict: these are the costs of culture and of the balance between reason and memory.

Index

Abbreviations: A. Aristotle; Sp. Spinoza.